Christianity and Society
in the Modern World

Series editors
HUGH McLEOD AND BOB SCRIBNER

The Jews in Christian Europe
1400–1700

The Jews in Christian Europe 1400–1700

JOHN EDWARDS

Routledge

LONDON AND NEW YORK

First published in 1988 by
Routledge
11 New Fetter Lane, London EC4P 4EE
29 West 35th Street, New York, NY 10001

Typeset in Great Britain by
Scarborough Typesetting Services
and printed by
T. J. Press (Padstow) Ltd
Padstow, Cornwall

British Library Cataloguing in Publication Data

Edwards, John, *1949–*
The Jews in Christian Europe. –
(Christianity and society in the modern world).
1. Europe. Jews, 1400–1700
I. Title.   II. Series
940.04924

ISBN 0-415-00864-6

Library of Congress Cataloging in Publication Data

Edwards, John, 1949–
The Jews in Christian Europe, 1400–1700/John Edwards.
p.   cm. – (Christianity and society in the modern world)
Bibliography: p.
Includes index.
ISBN 0-415-00864-6
1. Jews – Europe – History.   2. Judaism – Relations – Christianity.
3. Christianity and other religions – Judaism.
4. Jews-History – 70-1789.   5. Europe – Ethnic relations.
I. Title.   II. Series.
DS135.E81E38   1988
940′.004924 –dc19

To the memory of
W. W. Simpson
(1907–1987),

who worked for peace and for true understanding
between Christian
and Jew

I have my brothers among the Turks, Papists, Jews and all peoples. Not that they are Turks, Jews, Papists and Sectaries or will remain so; in the evening they will be called into the vineyard and given the same wage as we.

(Sebastian Franck)

Contents

Preface

Evidently, no historical work is written in a vacuum. Nevertheless, it is by no means certain that every historian will openly
admit his or her personal approach to the subject in hand. As
what follows can only be, by its very nature, a kind of essay on
Jewish life in Europe in the medieval fifteenth century and in the
so-called early modern period, that is between 1500 and 1700, it
is particularly necessary in this case to make clear from the start
what the work does, and does not, attempt to do, and to describe
its standpoint.

In the first place, it is no way a comprehensive survey, and still
less a monograph. It is therefore neither immensely detailed on a
small theme, nor all-inclusive in its subject matter. It is neither a
history of the Christian European society of the sixteenth and
seventeenth centuries, with Jews attached as some kind of
appendage, nor an exercise in Jewish history for its own sake. The
method employed in the book is more fully discussed in the
Introduction, but it is important to note at this stage that the
work attempts a two-way view of Christian and Jewish life, with a
stress on the relationships between adherents of the two faiths,
rather than on their separate, internal histories.

The writer's ability to provide such a perspective has, inevitably, some positive and some negative features. To begin with, a
grounding in the historical school of Oxford University, the later
influences of modern French and Spanish historical writing,
together with a lively and stimulating Medieval History
Department in Birmingham University, have all had their

effects, which are duly and gratefully acknowledged. In this context it is worth adding that no apology is made for the 'medieval' perspective of much of the text which follows. In addition, though, the book is written in a living Christian faith, and, in that sense, is neither dispassionate nor neutral. However, as its dedication indicates, it is also written on the contemporary 'frontier' between faiths, and particularly in the light of some years of dialogue and shared experience with Jews. Such activity has never been more urgently necessary than it is in the present century and, in this sense too, the following work is deeply-felt and committed.

It cannot, owing to the limitations of the author in both linguistic knowledge and personal experience, show an intimate or internal understanding of Jewish life, but the growing output of Jewish historians of the early modern period has been carefully considered and used as far as possible. In truth, though, the ancient and destructive division between Church and Synagogue is still, as much as it has ever been, in need of healing. It is hoped that the book will help, in a small way, to meet this desperate need.

Moseley, Birmingham,
on the Feast of the Nativity of
the Blessed Virgin Mary,
8 September, 1987, C.E.

Introduction:
From medieval to modern times?

The use of the phrase 'social history of religion' in itself suggests, in these complex times for historical writing, certain presuppositions about the meaning and explanation of the very term 'religion'. When the question at issue is the interrelationship between two distinct religious traditions or communities in a chronological period of two centuries, the matter becomes even more complicated, since the likelihood is that each will have its own view of the importance of that period and its place in that religion's perception of its own history. Both these difficulties will be major preoccupations throughout the pages which follow, but first it is necessary to define, as far as possible, the scope of the material which is to be discussed. The first possible conflict between Jewish and Christian perceptions arises at once, with the question of dating. Even the numbering of the year in which a given event took place involves certain fundamental religious affirmations. Since dating by regnal years is not a serious option, it is necessary to decide between the traditional Jewish date of the creation of the world by the Lord and the Christian date of the birth of Jesus Christ as the basic reference point. For practical purposes, however, the decision has already been made by the western dominance over the history of the world, which has been achieved, largely in a Christian tradition, over the last four or five hundred years. Therefore this discussion will concern the sixteenth and seventeenth centuries of the era dated from the supposed date of Jesus's birth, though this may be thought of, as has become a matter of Jewish convenience too, in terms of a 'Common' rather than a 'Christian' era.

Such a solution in itself indicates the major historical realities of the period and helps to define the geographical as well as the chronological scope of the work. In deference to the dominance which, by 1500, had been achieved by a form of Christianity which owed its origins and allegiance to Rome, the subject of the book will be the religious and social life of Jews and Christians in Catholic Europe, that is, the parts of the continent which both had Jewish populations in this period and were predominantly Catholic at its beginning. Thus the succeeding chapters will mainly be about Spain and Portugal, Italy and France, England, the Netherlands, the Holy Roman Empire, Poland, and Lithuania. They will be no more than marginally concerned with the eastern Mediterranean and Russia, or, in other words, the areas under Orthodox Christian or Muslim control. It will be noted that Jewish history in this period is here being defined in Christian terms. This seems to be a matter of simple historical reality, and does not presuppose any general view about the relative truth and strength of these two religions or the proper social relations between their adherents.

On the contrary, it is important to introduce at this stage a method of approach which will, it is hoped, allow both Christian and Jewish views of the period to be acknowledged. First of all, it is necessary to say that the general Christian, or post-Christian, perception of the sixteenth and seventeenth centuries today has little or no place in it for Jews. This popular view is reflected in virtually all the recent historical writing on the period which does not specifically concern itself with Jewish history. It is worth considering what this indicates about the actual role of Jews in Catholic Europe, which will be the subject of this book. For those in the 'Christian' tradition, which for this purpose includes agnostic and atheist historians too, the important events in the sixteenth and seventeenth centuries were the Renaissance and the more specifically religious Reformation, which between them broke up the old medieval institutional and cultural framework of Europe. There followed a period of violent and damaging conflict, at the end of which Europe was largely divided into two armed and religiously divergent camps. By 1600, medieval Europe had become early modern Europe, and the institutions of the historical profession, at all levels, still quite faithfully reflect this interpretation, which has survived the rejection by some practitioners of religion and culture as major historical factors, in favour of material social and economic phenomena. The latter part of the seventeenth century saw, according to this view, a further development of intellectual and cultural history, in which, in part as a reaction to the violence and disruption which was then perceived to have been caused by religion, new habits of thought were devised, first by a few brave and often persecuted individuals, and then by larger groups of increasingly influential people. This new mentality involved the rejection of irrational explanations of the phenomena of the world, including much of the intellectual edifice of organized Christianity, and, instead, a reliance on experiment and empirical observation as methods of understanding them. According to the conventional interpretation, the results of this intellectual change, which, by the eighteenth century is regarded as an Enlightenment, included the single-minded promotion of the perceived economic interests of states which is commonly known as mercantilism, a growth in official toleration of religious diversity, and, eventually, a type of enlightened absolute monarchy, known to eighteenth-century historians as enlightened despotism. If the Jews of Europe are fitted into this interpretation at all, then they are held to have benefited increasingly from all these phenomena, gaining greater religious, economic, and social freedom. Thus the sixteenth and seventeenth centuries are seen essentially as a period of transition from the break-up of most of the Jewish communities of western and central Europe to a new enlightened pattern of Jewish–Christian relations, in which Christian majorities abandon their old restrictions on Jewish life in return for an acceptance by Jews of the customs, and even the citizenship, of the Gentile majority. The Enlightenment thus destroys medieval Judaism as surely as it destroys medieval Catholicism.

Even when Christian dating is used, the Jewish perception of this period is very different, although Jewish historians in the nineteenth and twentieth centuries have on the whole been influenced by, or even helped to create, the historiographical movements which have affected their Gentile colleagues. In earlier times, however, there seems to have been little contact between Jews' and Christians' perceptions of their own history.

Lionel Kochan has argued that it is only in the sixteenth century that Jews began to take any interest in the histories of the Gentiles around them, and to include considerations of general history in their work. Before about 1500, and in part at least up to the eighteenth century, they concentrated on Jewish history alone, seeing it very much as a divine drama, worked out in Biblical terms and on an eternal time-scale, in the sense that salvation in religious terms was the purpose of human history, with the Jews having a special status among mankind as a result of their being chosen by God for a unique task of redemption.[1]

Such an approach meant, in historiographical terms, little or no attempt to understand the general situation in which Jews found themselves in various times and places, but rather a concentration on what Gentiles were doing or not doing to Jews in any given context. The Christians thus appear as somewhat arbitrary and mysterious outsiders, intervening from time to time in the internal history of Jewish communities, whose only aim was to be left alone to live according to Biblical and Talmudic, or rabbinical, principles and work out whatever purpose has been divinely ordained for them. Gentiles may from time to time have, Cyrus-like, an approved place in God's plan for the Jews, but a recognition of this role does not generally involve any serious interest in Gentile historical activity for its own sake. As is the case, to a large extent, with the development of Christian historiography, it is only in the so-called early modern period itself that Jews begin to take part in the intellectual developments going on in the majority communities around them, and 'modern' Jewish historiography begins to develop. From then on, it becomes less possible to distinguish a special methodological approach among Jewish historians. Instead, Jews adopt one commonly available to all scholars in the western world. Nevertheless, it is still important to notice, in modern work, which for this purpose means that of the nineteenth and twentieth centuries, some distinctive preoccupations which serve to mark off Jewish from Christian interpretations of the sixteenth and seventeenth centuries. In creating what has come to be known, rather unkindly, as the 'lachrymose' school of Jewish historiography, the great nineteenth-century historian Graetz and others have largely used modern historical techniques simply to continue the old passive Jewish approach to Gentile history. The story of the Jews thus continues to be, in part, that of what Gentiles have done or not done to the Jews.[2] However, in the nineteenth century and more recently, there have been other major preoccupations which significantly influence current Jewish perception of the history of the early modern period. The most important of these are both consequences of events since the end of the eighteenth century. Firstly, with the extension of greater freedom to Jews, particularly in France and Germany in the French Revolutionary and Napoleonic periods, the question of assimilation became a major issue in Judaism.[3] To what extent were Jews entitled to abandon religious and cultural practices from the past and still call themselves Jews? This question, together with the related issues of conversion and intermarriage with Gentiles, have been on the Jewish agenda ever since. Secondly, all these matters have been put in a wholly new perspective by the attempted systematic extermination by the Nazis of European Jewry. It is important for the non-Jewish reader to remember, at all times, that any consideration by Jews of the Jewish role in European history in earlier periods is likely today to be, to a greater or a lesser extent, consciously or unconsciously, governed by the experience, either personal or vicarious, of the Shoah or Holocaust. Thus the history of Jews in Catholic Europe in the sixteenth and seventeenth centuries is liable to be seen by Jewish commentators in a more defensive way than might have been the case before 1900, or even before 1939. The policies of Gentile governments will be judged by their willingness or otherwise to grant Jews life itself, and, as will become clearer in later chapters, those who adopted the option of assimilation will be liable to receive short shrift. The influence of recent events, including both the Holocaust and the establishment, in 1948, of an independent Jewish state for the first time since 70 AD CE, has not, of course, uniformly affected Jewish historians of Jewry, but the general interpretation of early modern Jewish history continues to see it as a period of readjustment following the late-medieval expulsion of communities from western Europe and preceding an 'assimilationist' episode which began in the late eighteenth century. According to this interpretation, the main activity of Jews in this period was to attempt to preserve their way

of life in the midst of the upheavals which did so much to change
or upset the Christian society in the midst of which they lived. An
exception to this view is the writing of Jonathan Israel, who
strongly urges that the sixteenth and seventeenth centuries
should be seen rather as a period of upheaval, and generally of
improvement, in the life of Jews in Catholic Europe.[4]

Israel's book, which appeared during the preparation of the
present work, covers much of the same chronological period and
subject matter, but from a different point of view. In the first
place, the author describes his work as 'essentially a secular
history which focuses on the changing patterns of political and
economic interaction between Europe's Jews and the states and
societies amongst which they dwelt'. There is a strong thesis
underlying his survey of Jews in the early modern period. It is
that, to some extent from 1500 onwards, and much more extensively after 1650, 'amid a flurry of new charters, privileges and
concessions, Jews were all at once released from many, though
admittedly by no means all, of the old, stifling restrictions on
their economic and cultural activity and lifestyle'. This change
came about as a result, firstly, of the break-up of Christendom
because of the Reformation, and secondly of the development,
from the late sixteenth century onwards, of mercantilist
economic policies and a non-ideological approach to government
and to relations between states, which is commonly described as
'*politique*'. For Israel, the result of this development for
Europe's Jews was to enable them to achieve 'the most profound
and pervasive impact on the west which they were ever to exert
whilst still retaining a large measure of social and cultural cohesion, that is to say, whilst still displaying a recognizably national
character'.

This thesis raises many questions, which the present work will
attempt to answer. Firstly, it is questionable whether a specifically
secular history, which avoids the inner development of religious
belief and practice, is feasible in the early modern period. It is
certainly arguable, as later chapters will show, that religion was
still as inextricably bound up with all other aspects of European
life in 1700 as it had been in 1500 – or indeed in 1200. Secondly,
it is doubtful in the extreme whether the customary early
modernist's assumption of a kind of *caesura* between the sixteenth

and previous centuries is any longer tenable as a basis for the study of history. The following chapters will make deliberate, explicit, and extensive reference to the medieval social history of Christians and Jews in Europe, in order to give a longer, and, it is suggested, more accurate perspective on early modern developments. This work will attempt to avoid dealing in religious, cultural, national, or economic monoliths, and will thus treat such concepts as 'the Jews', 'the Christians', 'the Church', or 'the Churches', and even 'the *politiques*' and 'mercantilism', with considerable caution and scepticism. The underlying thesis to be found in this work, therefore, is closer to the traditional view of continuity between the religious and social surroundings of medieval and early modern Jews. It is now time to look at the methods which will be used to produce a religious, not a secular social history of European Jewry in these centuries.[5]

In order to attempt to understand the social and religious life of Jews and Christians in the early modern period, it seems useful to establish, as far as possible, some relatively uncontroversial facts. It will therefore be necessary to ask how many Jews lived in each of the varied political units of the continent in this period, where exactly they lived and in what conditions, whether or not they were confined to a ghetto and what occupations they were able to exercise. The answers to these questions, where they are obtainable, will go a long way towards indicating the social and economic place of Jews among the Christian majority. As will become clear, the available materials do not always supply easy, or indeed any, answers. It is almost never possible to provide exact population figures in this period, either for Jews or for Christians. Early modern bureaucratic practice makes it far more usual for household numbers to be recorded than numbers of individuals, and, in the case of Jews, such records, which were normally compiled for taxation purposes, often go no further than indicating the existence of whole communities, from which global sums were demanded. It may be possible to suggest, as Salo Baron has done, that demographic movements among Jewish communities may have differed somewhat from these of their Gentile neighbours, owing to the strict dietary practices and lower marriage age of the Jews, but these must still, with the existing knowledge of population statistics and trends, remain essentially subjective and unquantifiable assertions.[6] It is, however, possible to say something about the role of Jews in the general economy and society and thus about their public relations with the majority communities.

The proper historical treatment of religious experience is an even more subtle and difficult problem, and before Jewish and Christian religious life may in this respect be compared, it is necessary to establish some criteria for describing and assessing what seems to have happened. In the process, the prejudices, assumptions, and predilections of the author will inevitably be exposed, at least in part. To begin with, it may be useful to consider religious phenomena, or those which were so described by participants, in three main categories, which inevitably and constantly overlap and interrelate. The first of these is what may be called 'official' religion. This includes not only the thought, writings, and teaching of religious leaderships but also the activities of their political supporters. Religious authority thus merges, in the context of the attempt to assure adherence by subject populations to a certain prescribed model of belief and practice, with what is generally called secular or state authority. The extent to which such authorities succeeded in controlling the activities of large numbers of people will be a constant theme among both Jews and Christians. The second important category to be borne in mind is one which has come to greater prominence in recent years, largely as a result of the historical work of the *Annales* school of Marc Bloch and Lucien Febvre, and, partly through its mediation, of the disciplines of anthropology, ethnology, and sociology. This is what may be called social, public, or corporate religion. The subject matter of this aspect of religious phenomena involves not only public worship in synagogues and churches, but also the whole 'sacred landscape', to use William A. Christian's phrase,[7] of shrines, images, and holy places, which was a particular feature of late medieval Christianity and which also to some extent affected Jews and Muslims who lived on the European mainland. In addition, the phenomena of social religion include, for this purpose, the pilgrimages, processions, and other public rituals which were so prominent a part of sixteenth- and seventeenth-century life, and which were by no means the sole property of the Catholic faith.* Thirdly, it will be impossible to ignore the individual religious experience of Jews and Christians. This is, of course, the category for which it is most difficult to obtain evidence. However, it cannot be discounted because it seems clear, from materials emanating from various parts of Europe (which will be considered in due course) that so many variations on the officially prescribed patterns of religious belief and practice were to be found in this period that a conservative and cautious refusal to consider the scattered and often intractable evidence would result in the conveying of a seriously misleading impression of what actually seems to have been going on. At this stage, it is necessary to do no more than give one example of the kind of phenomena which would remain inexplicable without a willingness to consider individual religious experience. This is the issue of conversion from Judaism to Christianity, which, partly for reasons which have already been suggested, is probably the aspect of Jewish experience in the early modern period which still excites the most interest and causes the most soul-searching and even distress. As will become clear, particularly in chapters 1 and 4, this phenomenon inevitably brings into play all the factors which have just been outlined. It seems that no realistic, let alone comprehensive, understanding of the '*converso* condition' is possible unless general concepts such as 'the *converso*' are broken down into the individuals which made them up. It is appropriate, therefore, that the story should start with Spain, where government decisions, taken in the late fifteenth century, created problems for both Christians and Jews during the succeeding centuries.[8]

Notes

1 Lionel Kochan, *The Jew and his History*, London, Macmillan, 1977, pp. 1–34.
2 ibid., pp. 69–87.
3 See, for example, Jacob Katz, *Out of the Ghetto. The Social Background of Jewish Emancipation, 1770–1870*, New York, Schocken Books, 1978.
4 Jonathan I. Israel, *European Jewry in the Age of Mercantilism, 1550–1750*, Oxford, Clarendon Press, 1985, esp. pp. 1–3, 252–9.
5 ibid., pp. v, 1–4, 258.

* Such studies are indeed beginning to remodel the traditional political interpretation of early modern Europe.

6 Salo Wittmayer Baron, *A Social and Religious History of the Jews, Late Middle Ages and Era of European Expansion, 1200–1650*, vol. xvi, *Poland–Lithuania, 1500–1650*, New York/Philadelphia, Columbia University Press, Jewish Publication Society of America, 1976, pp. 199–204.

7 William A. Christian, Jr, *Local Religion in Sixteenth-century Spain*, Princeton, Princeton University Press, 1981, esp. pp. 175–7.

8 For a fuller discussion of this method of analysis, see John Edwards, 'The *conversos*: a theological approach', *Bulletin of Hispanic Studies*, lxii (1985), 39–49.

1

Jewish expulsion and dispersion from Spain

Although the greatest historical attention has, with good reason, been focused on the expulsion of unbaptized Jews from Spain in 1492 and from Portugal in 1497, these acts were only the most prominent among many which had the effect of almost removing a Jewish presence from western Europe. The Jewish experience of the sixteenth and seventeenth centuries is incomprehensible without an awareness of the events of the later Middle Ages and of the theoretical and practical attitudes towards Jews which had been evolved before 1500 by Christians of all social levels. The concept of expelling whole Jewish communities from kingdoms or other states itself evolved from a long period of co-existence between adherents of the two religions on the European continent. Once the first such decision had been taken, by Edward I of England, in 1290, there followed a gradual extension of the principle to other areas, the initiative finally coming from rulers themselves. The Capetian Philip IV attempted to expel Jews from the French territories under his control in 1306, and a further effort was made by his Valois successors in 1394. The social, economic, and political upheavals of the fourteenth century, including warfare and the natural catastrophe of the Black Death, led to pressure and restriction on the remaining Jewish communities in France, Germany, and Spain because of the widespread accusation that Jews were responsible for the spread of the plague. But 'definitive' expulsions only became widespread in the first half of the fifteenth century, beginning in Vienna in 1421 and continuing with Linz in the same year,

Cologne in 1424, Augsburg in 1439, Bavaria in 1442, with a second attempt in 1450, and the royal cities of Moravia in 1454. The piecemeal implementation of the expulsion policy in the Holy Roman Empire reflects the fragmented nature of that political entity in the period. Between 1490 and 1510, Jews were expelled from Geneva, Mecklenburg, Pomerania, Halle, Magdeburg, Lower Austria, Styria, Carinthia, Württemberg, the archdiocese of Salzburg, Nuremberg, Ulm, and the electorate of Brandenburg. Local expulsions also occurred in Italy, at Perugia in 1485, Vicenza in 1486, Parma in 1488, Milan and Lucca in 1489, and Florence and its subject towns in 1494. The Spanish expulsion also spilled over into Spanish-ruled territories in Italy, including Sardinia and Sicily in the same year, 1492, and, once Ferdinand had regained Naples from the French in 1510, most of the Jews on the mainland south of Rome were expelled too. In 1498, the French Crown finally achieved a long-term aim by removing Jews from its lands in Provence.[1] The shift of the centre of gravity of Jewish life in Europe from the west of the continent to the centre and east will be one of the major themes of what follows. It is necessary first, though, to examine the process which led to such remarkable unanimity among the rulers of Europe, apart from the Popes, who allowed Jews to remain in their Italian and French territories, and those who controlled comparatively few other lesser political units.

The medieval Church and the Jews

Religious tension between the Jews and Christians is of the essence of the origins of Christianity itself. A conflict seems to have arisen inevitably from the historical priority of Judaism and the fact that Christianity first broke away from it and then achieved vastly greater power and influence. These two phenomena created a fundamental imbalance in the relationship between the two religions and their adherents in later centuries. In the first place, Jews needed much less from religious dialogue, for its own sake, than did Christians. In theological terms, it was the Christians who needed to justify, to themselves as much as to anyone else, their rebellion against Judaism and their subsequent independence. They needed Jews to admit that this rebellion had in fact been justified, and to end the schism by accepting the Christian revelation. Jews, on the other hand, had no special need for religious dialogue as such. As has already been stated in the earlier discussion of historical perceptions, medieval Jews believed that they already had the truth and a divinely ordained role in the world's history. In religious terms, they had nothing to learn from Christians. In political, social, and economic terms, on the other hand, the situation was very different. Quite early in the independent history of Christianity, and certainly by the fourth century, when the Emperor Constantine converted to that religion and officially adopted it throughout his empire, the Christian theological attitude to Judaism had begun to inter-relate with social policy towards Jews. Theory was beginning to influence practice. Although the authorship and redaction of the texts which came eventually to be regarded as the canonical New Testament is a subject of deep doubt and controversy, it is un-deniable that the versions which were handed down as the revealed word of God to medieval Christians, in the Latin Vulgate translation, already contained words which theologically condemned and downgraded Judaism and which could, if turned into practical policy, have had a similar effect on the persons of Jews themselves. Thus the apostle Paul, in the midst of his pastoral controversies with non-Christian and Christian Jews, often resorted to strong language in his letters. Writing to the Corinthians, for example, he said: 'Their minds were hardened; for to this day, when they read the old covenant, the same veil remains unlifted, because only through Christ is it taken away. Yet to this day whenever Moses is read a veil lies over their minds' (2 Cor. 3: 14–16). This passage includes the motifs of blindness and hardness of heart which were to become stock attributes of Jews in the minds of medieval Christians and which were to be faithfully repeated in the Good Friday collect in Cranmer's Anglican prayer book, still 'legal tender' today, in its 1662 version. Some Gospel passages, probably written later in the first century, although this is very much a matter of dispute, go even further in providing ideas and vocabulary for Christian hostility to Jews. This is particularly true of John's gospel, through its varied and undiscriminating use of the phrase 'the Jews' to mean, at different times, the Jewish political leadership, religious parties or sects, such as the Pharisees and Sadducees, or even the people as a whole.[2] When Jesus said to the Pharisees, according to John's account, 'You are of your father the devil; and your will is to do your father's desires. He was a murderer from the beginning, and has nothing to do with the truth' (John 8: 44), it seems hardly surprising that the ignorant, or the malicious, should have assumed these words to apply to all Jews, both past and contemporary.

Although good recent scholarship suggests, contrary to what some Christian theologians have thought in the guilt-laden period since the Holocaust, that it would be quite wrong to assume that anti-Jewish feeling did not exist in the Ancient World before the rise of Christianity,[3] it cannot be denied that, in the medieval period, scriptural teaching, as interpreted by the Church, came to have a considerable influence on secular policy towards the Jews. In the seventh century, the apparent power vacuum in Visigothic Spain allowed Church councils, meeting in Toledo, to attempt to put into practice the anti-Jewish sentiments which had previously remained in the minds and written work of the Fathers. The success of these measures was very probably slight, even before they were overtaken and obliterated by the Muslim invasion and conquest, but they at least threatened economic and social persecution, as well as heavy pressure to convert to Christianity.[4] However, it was in the eleventh century that European Jews under Christian rule once again found themselves subject to large-scale persecution.

He Who spoke causing the world to come into being – He shall avenge the spilt blood of His servants. The enemy said: 'Let us take to ourselves possession of the habitations of God,' and 'Let us cut them off from being a nation; that the name of Israel may be no more in remembrance.'[5]

The late medieval history of the Jews in western Europe may be held to begin with the attacks on Jewish communities in the Rhineland mounted by forces taking part in the First Crusade. In the spring and summer of 1096, large but unknown numbers of Jews were murdered by the followers of Emicho of Leiningen, and probably in some cases by local inhabitants in Mainz, Cologne,

Speyer, Worms, and many other places. A group of chronicles, or martyrologies as Kochan has described them in the case of an account of the similar massacres which took place in the Second Crusade, has survived.[6] Although the literary relation between the three main sources, the chronicles of Bar Simson and of Rabbi Eliezer bar Nathan, together with the *Narrative of the Old Persecutions*, or *Mainz Anonymous*, is not entirely clear, they all appear to be twelfth-century compositions, intended not to give a historical account as such, but rather to provide a liturgical and religious commentary and commemoration to indicate to later Jewish communities the persecutions which might await them and the patterns of behaviour which would be expected of them in such circumstances. As such, they are characteristic of Jewish self-perception throughout the late medieval period, but they are also interesting because of the motives which they ascribe to their Christian opponents. As in the above quotation from Bar Simson, these are held by the Jewish writers to be both economic and religious. Jews were robbed of their wealth, but they were also faced, on numerous occasions, with the choice between baptism and death, and the authors of the chronicles of the First and Second Crusades held up the example of the Rhineland communities to their successors because so many, in 1096, chose to die, often by their own hands, rather than convert.[7] This example was, however, to be rarely followed in later centuries. It is interesting also to note the contemporary Christian reaction to the massacres and mass suicides of the Jews. Christian chronicles of the Crusades generally have little or no space for these events, though Albert of Aix gives a brief account, critical of Christian conduct, of the deaths in Cologne and Mainz.[8] It seems fairly clear, though, that whatever the motives of these attacks, they received no kind of official approval, ecclesiastical or secular.

This situation appears to change in the thirteenth century, thus forming the religious, political and social context in which most of western Europe's Jews were to find themselves up to the sixteenth century. It is best to set out the general policies which were proposed, before attempting to understand the rationale and motives behind them. The most important single influence on secular policy towards Jews in the later Middle Ages, other than more immediate and local factors, was the Fourth Lateran

Council of the Roman Church, which, in 1215, produced guide-
lines on Christian conduct towards Jews intended to be manda-
tory for all the faithful, including the rulers of states, who were to
embody them in their own legislation and enforce them as soon
and as effectively as possible. One purpose of this legislation was
to reduce social contact between Jews and Christians. Ideally, the
only dealings allowed would be economic transactions between
specialized merchants and traders of the two communities. There
should be no sexual relations between partners of differing religions. Jews were not to employ Christians or to hold any kind of
public office which would give them authority over Christians. In
addition, Jewish worship was to be restricted. Maintenance of
existing synagogues was to be permitted, but new ones were not
normally to be built, and, if they were, they should certainly not
be elaborate or ornate in design. There is no specific demand for
ghettos in Lateran IV, but the Church's laws clearly supposed a
large effective measure of segregation.[9] The enthusiasm and
effectiveness with which rulers attempted to enforce these laws in
their own countries varied considerably, as will become clear, but
at this stage it is important to consider why a religious body such
as the Roman Church should have legislated in this way on
matters of social policy.

The first point to notice is that the Lateran IV canons were not
original in their content. The seventh-century Visigothic councils
of Toledo, already mentioned, had gone considerably further.
The difference was that, in taking up the old question of the
proper relationship between Christians and the Jewish communities in their midst, the fathers of Lateran IV were legislating
for the whole of the western Church. If their plans were
implemented by secular rulers, they would therefore have considerable influence on the life of the continent. The question of
what they were hoping to achieve by these measures is not, however, altogether simple to answer. In an important recent book,
Jeremy Cohen has argued that the thirteenth century saw a significant change in the Church's policy towards the Jews, one which
is reflected not only in the 1215 legislation but also in the work of
the orders of mendicant friars, which began and rapidly developed
in the rest of the thirteenth century and beyond. Neither of these
points can be accepted without careful consideration, which

should begin with Christian theology concerning relations between Christians and Jews. For reasons which have already been suggested, much medieval Christian concern with Judaism, certainly in the period between the seventh and thirteenth centuries, was rooted in the pages of the Bible, rather than social relations with contemporary Jews. There were, however, two traditional views of the theological role of Jews, if this were to correspond to God's plan. The assumption of all thoughtful Christians, and of many others more given to riot than to theological argument, was that eventually all Jews would have to become Christian. Their religion had become obsolete as soon as Jesus began his earthly ministry, so that later Jews were no more than stubborn adherents of a 'fossilized' religion. It will become clear, in due course, that such a view would by no means disappear at the end of the Middle Ages, but, for the moment, it is necessary to consider the problem with which medieval Christians believed themselves to be faced. What, if anything, was to be 'done' with the Jews? Opinions were divided, mainly on the question of time-scale. Although the long-term aim of including all Jews within the Church was shared almost universally by clerical and lay Christians, it was not clear how or when this should be done. It was generally agreed that the mass conversion of the Jews would be, as stated in the last book of the New Testament, the Revelation of St John the Divine (or the Apocalypse as most medieval Christians knew it), one of the events which heralded the end of the world and the Last Judgement, so vividly portrayed on the walls of many churches. It will be clear from this that the treatment of the Jews was very likely to become entangled with thinking about eschatology, or the study of the 'last days'. In fact, in the later Middle Ages and on into the sixteenth and seventeenth centuries, policies and attitudes towards the Jews depended to a considerable extent on when particular rulers and churchmen believed the apocalypse was likely to take place. One school of thought, which Cohen links with the name of Augustine of Hippo, made little effort to predict the date when the last days would begin, taking into account Jesus's request, as recorded in Mark, Matthew, and Luke's gospels, not to attempt to 'know the times or the seasons'.[10] An historical scheme which envisaged an indefinite wait for the conversion of the Jews did not encourage active missionary work. Thus the Augustinian view assumed that, for the foreseeable future, Jews would remain, unconverted, among the Christian majority in Europe. Their right to do so could not be questioned, but, in order to ensure that they did not attract Christians away from the true faith, whether by means of religious proselytism or by economic pressures or personal ties, they were to be restricted to a subordinate and economically less successful social role. Thus, while the consummation of all things was awaited, Jewish communities would remain as a visible warning of what happened to those who deviated from Christian orthodoxy. It was neither necessary nor desirable, however, to convert them immediately, and it was certainly wrong to expel them. It must be clear that the provisions of the Fourth Lateran Council stand fairly and squarely within this tradition, which therefore became the ideal model for all provinces of the Church and all secular authorities in their policies towards Jews in the late Middle Ages, and, in the case of the Papacy, in the succeeding centuries.

There was, however, another interpretation of eschatology which led to a much more active Christian policy towards the Jews. The fundamental difference between this and the Augustinian view is that the former assumed the last days to be calculable and likely to occur before long. Such a view made the whole question of preparing for the second coming of Christ much more urgent, and the conversion of the Jews a high priority. If put into practice, it would lead to large-scale missionary work among the Jews, and even efforts to force them to be baptized. Strong feelings arose at different times throughout the Middle Ages, and among all social classes, that the end of the world was near. Commonly, such phenomena were connected either with significant dates in the Christian calendar, such as the beginnings of millennia or of new centuries, or else with major catastrophes such as the Black Death of 1348–51. On the whole, though, 'millenarian' movements, as they have come to be known, have not gained official approval.[11] It seems that the mighty spiritual upsurge which followed Pope Urban II's famous call to crusade at Clermont in late 1095 contained a significant element of such sentiment, related to the approaching year 1100, and stimulated by the chance, suddenly offered, to be physically present in the Holy City, Jerusalem, where both Jews and Christians believed the events of the end of time would begin.[12] It may well be that the Rhineland Jews fell victim, not only to economic greed but also to a degree of millenarian sentiment. However, it is only, according to Cohen's argument, in the thirteenth century that any official Church organization adopted an active missionary policy, soon to be followed, in the case of Edward I's England, by the first European case of the expulsion of a whole community which refused to convert. The groups to which the major role in this change of policy and action is ascribed are the newly founded orders of friars, in particular the Franciscans and Dominicans. The evidence to support this view seems strong. The friars were active preachers, especially the Dominicans who existed for this sole purpose, and there is no doubt that they saw conversion of the Jews as one of their main tasks. Franciscans and Dominicans took a leading role in formal theological 'disputations' such as those in Paris in 1240 and Barcelona in 1263.[13] They set up 'houses of converts' to ease the transition of former Jews into Christian society by separating them from their former co-religionaries and preventing them from suffering economic loss as well, during the change.[14] Their attempts, especially in the case of the Franciscans, to bring the Christian laity more fully into the liturgical life of the Church included the development of active Lenten and Passion devotions which raised religious fervour and might easily focus attention, often leading to violent hostility, on the local Jewish community. Such phenomena occurred all over Catholic Europe on many occasions in the later Middle Ages. The friars also provided most of the inquisitors, once the specialized Inquisition was developed, from the 1230s onwards.

None the less, doubts must remain concerning any theory which simplistically ascribes the blame for the deterioration in the conditions of life of many Jews in the late Middle Ages to the friars. First, the debate between the Augustinian and the more radical view of eschatology should not be seen as placing the friars on one side and the traditional Church hierarchy on the other. The mendicant orders were radical, but they were none the less increasingly incorporated into the mainstream of institutional Christianity, of which they had always in reality been a part. As

their expertise grew with the help of converts and of their experience as preachers, ministers to the urban laity, and inquisitors,
the friars developed a more complex view of the Judaism which
confronted them. The starting point of this process was the assumption that, up to Jesus's birth on earth, the Jews had had a
valid place in the divine plan for mankind. Up to that point, the
Jews were indeed the Chosen People, as they themselves still
claimed, and their Law, or Torah, was divinely sanctioned.
However, in Jesus, God had replaced the Torah with a new 'law
of grace', embodied in the Saviour himself. The problem was
that Judaism did not in fact finish at that point, but continued to
develop, after the exile of the Jews from Palestine in the first
century. This development took the form of what came to be
known as rabbinical Judaism, with its own written texts, the
Talmud, which were believed to be part of the Law given to
Moses on Mount Sinai but at that stage only spoken by God to
Moses and not written down. The Talmud, with its diverse
content of legal commentaries, stories, and rabbinical discussions, provided the real framework for medieval Jewish life at all
levels, from the highest theology to the most mundane features
of daily existence. It was in the thirteenth century that Christians
first began to appreciate the importance of the Talmud, with the
help of friars who had converted from Judaism. Two such were
Nicholas Donin and Pablo Christiani, who played a leading role
in organizing the formal disputations at Paris and Barcelona,
respectively. In Louis IX's France, the Talmud was condemned
out of hand, as not being part of the Law and as containing evil
counsel and blasphemies against Christianity. Such views were
based on Pope Gregory IX's 1233 condemnation of the Talmud,
which he claimed to identify as the source of the anti-social
behaviour of contemporary Jews.[15] Although a more
sophisticated and selective approach was adopted by the
Dominicans in Barcelona in 1263, Gregory IX's attitude was to
form the basis of the Church's approach to the Jews on many
occasions in the late medieval and early modern periods.

There is, however, an important general issue which arises out
of Cohen's close identification of the friars with new attitudes to
Jews from the thirteenth century onwards. In this case, as in the
whole of the discussion of Christian–Jewish relations which

follows, it is vital not to fall into the trap of treating the subject as though it were isolated from other events around it. Perhaps because of the considerable involvement of theologians in the study of the history of Christianity's attitude to Judaism, or else because of the deeply ingrained habit among Jews of identifying as completely as possible with the fate of their co-religionaries in whatever period, a very great deal of the recent material on the subject appears to lack a sense of historical dynamic or historical context. The danger of this attitude is that it can easily lead to the unconscious assumption that Christianity and Judaism are unchanged and unchanging monoliths engaged in some kind of teleological relationship. Theology lends itself to such an approach, but this method will not do as a way of studying history. The case of the development of the Fourth Lateran Council's programme for the treatment of the Jews in Catholic Europe is the first of many to be considered here, in which the whole context will have to be examined. The most important point to notice is that the orders of friars did not originate with the intention of confronting or converting Jews, but rather out of a religiously-motivated desire to reform Christianity from within, although they also quickly became involved in the repression of heresy inside the Church. Similarly, while it is widely believed, because of the Spanish experience, that the Inquisition was an anti-Jewish organization, such a view is also untrue. The 'Holy Office' developed during the papal reign of Gregory IX, in order to repress the dualist Cathar heresy and the rebellious, lay Waldensian movement in southern France and northern Italy. The new tribunal had, in canon law, no jurisdiction over non-Christians, though, incredibly in the eyes of later scholars, one faction of Jews in southern France did, in the early days of the Inquisition, invite it to intervene in an internal Jewish conflict over the views of the philosopher, theologian, and physician Maimonides.[16] By the fourteenth century, when the Catalan inquisitor Nicholas Eymerich compiled his *Inquisitors' Manual*, which was still current in a revised form in the early modern period, the tribunal had developed a doctrine which permitted the investigation and trial of unbaptized Jews by the Holy Office.[17] It evolved from the new interest in the Talmud, drawing a strong distinction between rabbinical Judaism, which was condemned out of hand, and Old Testament Judaism, which at least contained a grain of Christian truth. The conclusion drawn by Eymerich and his colleagues was that inquisitors were entitled to intervene in Jewish affairs in order to punish those who rejected the common beliefs of Christians and Jews, such as the creation story, the unity of God and the ten commandments. It remains to be seen how far this policy was implemented.

Christian attitudes to Jews in the late Middle Ages were not, however, the sole preserve of church leaders, inquisitors, and secular rulers. Out of a combination of garbled and exaggerated versions of church teaching and secular laws, there developed a series of myths and stories which had currency among all classes and, at one time or another, in all parts of Catholic Europe. In general terms, the theological view of the Jews as obstinate adherents of a dead religion, as inveterate enemies of Christianity, and as a threat to the rest of the population, moved from the written texts of the theologians, the inquisitors, and the lawyers, first into iconography and then into concrete accusations of crimes, which on occasions led to further violence, robbery, and even deaths. The power of the visual image is now properly recognized as a major influence on human conduct, not only in the Middle Ages but also in later periods. In the case of the portrayal of Jews by Gentile artists, the desired religious and social image was portrayed not only in illustrations to manuscripts, but also, more publicly, in ecclesiastical sculpture and painting. A visual characterization of contemporary Jews was evolved in all countries. Although the Jewish religion, as a theological abstraction, was conventionally portrayed as a blind female figure, in contrast to the more beautiful and clear-sighted Church, most pictures show male Jews, often in the distinctive hats and badges worn at different times and in different places at the request of Lateran IV and later secular rulers, in order to make it easier for Christians to avoid dealings with adherents of the old religion.

The question of the physical appearance of medieval and early modern Jews has, of course, implications which go far beyond iconography. The Church decreed that secular rulers should make their Jewish subjects wear badges. These were generally wheel-shaped, and coloured either red or yellow, but they were sometimes a combination of the two. In other cases, specially designed hats, conical or otherwise pointed, had to be worn. The purpose may simply have been punitive, to indicate the inferior and isolated status of the Jew in accordance with traditional theology. It could, however, have been due to the fact that Jews could not otherwise be visually distinguished from Christians, when outside their specifically Jewish context, for example while travelling and doing business. There is no doubt, as Bernhard Blumenkranz has shown in a comprehensive study, that a Jewish stereotype existed in Christian art in this period. The Jew was given a hooked nose, while his hair was commonly dark and his complexion swarthy.[18] As Trachtenberg has shown too, he might also acquire diabolical attributes, such as horns and a horribly distorted countenance, visually representing the words from John's gospel already quoted.[19] However, in the cases of northern France, Spain, Germany, and Italy, it is possible to check such evidence against the Jews' own portrayal of themselves. Although human figures might not appear in religious art, it was customary in certain times and places for the illuminations of Hebrew manuscripts to show scenes from Jewish life. These might include religious ceremonies at home and in synagogue, business, travel, and even, in the case of late medieval Germany, flight from persecution. The picture could hardly be more different from that provided by the Christians. Of course, no Jew would portray another as a devil, but what is more striking is that badges and special hats almost never appear, even in contexts in which the law certainly required them to be worn. Instead, although there may be some difference in physical appearance between northern European Jews and their Christian contemporaries, this was really very slight, and scarcely seems to have existed at all in the pictures from fourteenth-century Spain and fifteenth-century Italy. Apart from using religious objects such as prayer-shawls, Jews seem, from this account, to have seen themselves as largely indistinguishable from their Christian contemporaries.[20]

The social implications of such ideological and visual stereotyping were to haunt Jewish communities in Catholic Europe throughout the late Middle Ages and on into the early modern period. Like Christian heretics, such as Cathars, or groups suffering from much-feared diseases, such as lepers, Jews

were liable to be blamed for all social ills. They were accused of
plotting the downfall of Christendom, and one complex fantasy,
the great 'leper conspiracy' in France in 1321, managed to
include all these categories at the same time, adding the Muslim
king of Granada for good measure, as an outside sponsor.[21]
Accusations of Jewish crime and anti-social behaviour centred at
all times on the occupations which were perceived by the
Christian majority to be most typical of Jews, in other words,
money-lending and medicine. However, there were also, from
time to time, upsurges of anti-Jewish feeling which normally
arose out of natural disasters such as plague; the Black Death of
1348–51, together with its succeeding epidemics, being the most
notorious example. In time of plague, Jews were accused of
sending their doctors to poison Christians, members of the upper
classes in particular, who commonly employed them. They were
even charged with poisoning the water supplies, managing to
escape death themselves either by greater hygiene or by magic,
both methods, even simple cleanliness, having a diabolical
aspect in the minds of Christians. However, perhaps the most
significant accusations made against Jews in this period
concerned the abuse of Christianity and the murder, for ritual
purposes, of Christian children.

A great deal of the stereotyping of Jews by Christians which has
been described so far clearly involves the inversion of Christian
practices and values. The whole 'diabolization' of the Jew as a
religious and social being is an example of this process, and it is
hardly surprising that the main devotion of the Catholic Church,
the Eucharist or Mass, should have become associated with
accusations against the Jews. The central moment in the Mass,
the focus of a great deal of Christian religious feeling, was the
conversion in the hands of a duly ordained priest of the unleavened bread into the body of the Saviour. Although theologians might attempt to analyse this change in philosophical terms,
it was inevitable that the miraculous aspect of the rite should
have led to a belief of the faithful, and not necessarily only of the
uneducated, that magic was involved. The use of the concept of
magic in the medieval and early modern periods will be
considered in due course, but the significant point here is that it
was assumed that Jews like Christians, would be interested in

using the consecrated host for magical purposes. The Jews, however, being 'servants of the devil', in Christian eyes, would naturally use it solely for evil aims. Thus the common ecclesiastical fear of abuse of the host by Christians, which led to the locking away in tabernacles of consecrated bread for future use, was extended into accusations, on many occasions in the late Middle Ages, that Jews were stealing hosts for use in their own rituals.

In Christian beliefs concerning the fate of the stolen hosts, eucharistic doctrine easily merged with the supposed diabolic nature of the Jews to produce stories of host-torture, in which the body of Christ was once again tormented by the Jews. They were so routinely blamed for Jesus's death, and thus for the murder of God, that often in late medieval art the Roman soldiers at the crucifixion were portrayed as stereotyped examples of contemporary, medieval Jews.[22] Increased knowledge of Jewish religious practices, gained largely from converts and from the Inquisition's work, led to the belief that Jews would use the stolen bread, or the blood extracted from it, in their Passover meal, or *seder* – from which, according to the New Testament, the Eucharist itself in any case derived. However, the development of the Christian myth did not stop there. Although Catholic Christians believed the consecrated host to be the actual body of Christ, there was no doubt that the core of Christian devotion, which, as has already been noted, was stressed ever more among the laity in the late Middle Ages, was the incarnation, passion, death, and resurrection of Jesus himself. The Jews' part in Christ's death thus came to be repeated, in the minds of medieval Christians, in the 'ritual murder' accusation, which had atrocities done by Jews to a Christian child, generally a young boy, instead of to a consecrated host. Accusations of mysterious and murderous rites had been made by pagans in the Ancient World against both Jews and, ironically, Christians, probably as a result of inadequate understanding of Passover and eucharistic rituals. But the late medieval Christian accusations began in England in 1144, when a child called William was found dead in Thorpe wood, on the outskirts of Norwich. According to the chronicler Thomas of Monmouth, who wrote the history of the consequent cult, the boy was murdered by local Jews, in accordance with an agreement among international Jewry that a Christian child should be killed each year, so that his blood might be used to make Passover bread. Despite the reluctance of royal officials to believe the story, a cult quickly grew in the cathedral priory. The ritual murder accusation, or 'blood libel', recurred from time to time between then and the end of the Middle Ages, wherever a child was lost or met his death – the victims always being male – in an area where there was a Jewish community. As in Norwich, the initial and subsequent attitudes of the ecclesiastical and secular authorities were always a vital factor in the development of such incidents, one of which, that of the so-called 'holy child of La Guardia', was to play an important part in the decision to expel the Jews from Spain.[23]

The Spanish expulsion was a great shock, not only to the affected individuals, but also to Jewry as a whole. It will be seen that the results were to be psychological as well as physical, and the degree of amazement which greeted the Catholic Monarchs' pragmatic, or decree, of 3 March 1492 indicates the strong and previously secure position that Jews had achieved in late medieval Spain. The argument for saying that the Spanish communities were the most flourishing in Europe up until the fifteenth century is based not so much on the large size of the Jewish population as on the range of economic and social roles which it was allowed to occupy. The actual population numbers will be discussed shortly, but it is important to note at the outset that the Spanish communities had a quite fully-developed social structure, which included aristocratic elements, religious and economic élites, artisans, and even farmers.

The legal basis on which Jewish life rested in Spain was similar in theory to that which existed in other countries, but the social climate was special to Spain, and also to Portugal, which had achieved a separate political identity in the mid-twelfth century. The main reasons for this distinctiveness were the eighth-century Muslim invasion, the subsequent spasmodic efforts by Christians to regain control over all the lands of the Peninsula, and the consequent fact that Judaism was not the only religious minority in the Iberian kingdoms, in contrast with the rest of Europe where Jews had that unique role. In addition, the Spanish church and secular rulers had developed, in the early and High Middle Ages, a considerable independence in their approach to papal legislation. Thus while, as elsewhere in Europe, the Jews were legally the serfs or slaves of the various Peninsular rulers, there was a great reluctance to enforce the canons of the Fourth Lateran Council, and, although current Church teaching was incorporated into the *Siete partidas*, the seven-part law code of Alfonso X of Castile, this itself was not promulgated with legal force until 1348, nearly a century after its composition. In practice, some Jews were allowed to exercise authority over Christians, as tax-farmers and collectors. Others were allowed to hold land and often worked it. Business and social relations between Jews and Christians were clearly frequent, both in the bigger and the smaller towns.

All was not well however. Most of Spain, and especially Catalonia, suffered from the Black Death in the mid-fourteenth century, though Portugal seems largely to have escaped. Exact losses cannot be calculated because of limited evidence, but it is probable that the worst-affected areas suffered the loss of between a third and a half of their population. As Miguel Angel Ladero Quesada has suggested, there is no reason to suppose that Jewish communities suffered more or less than their Gentile neighbours, despite popular myths on the subject. There is little doubt, however, that it was the period of the Black Death which began the definitive decline of Spanish Jewry, though this would certainly not have been apparent at the time. The epidemic was, none the less, followed by a period of social and economic dislocation and political instability throughout the Peninsula. In particular, all social classes attempted as far as they could to exploit the new circumstances at the expense of the rest of society. In addition, war broke out between Castile and Aragon, involving, in due course, not only the other Peninsular kingdoms but also the major combatants of the Hundred Years' War, England and France. In Castile, there was a civil war which resulted in the deposition and murder of the king, Peter, and his replacement by his illegitimate half-brother, Henry II. The latter founded a dynasty known as the Trastamarans which came to an end with the death of Ferdinand in 1516. Henry had depended for support on an alliance with the French, on the forces supplied by dissident nobles, and also on a policy of hostility to the Jews. Having achieved definitive victory in 1369, he rewarded his aristocratic allies with largesse in the form of Crown lands, vassals, public offices, and tax revenues, but he also attempted, through the parliament, or Cortes, to enforce the Lateran Council's programme more effectively. The early Trastamarans quickly found that it was impossible to operate the royal taxation system without the help of Jewish financiers, but there is no doubt that pressure on Jewish communities was building up, not only in Castile but also in the Crown of Aragon, in the last three decades of the fourteenth century.

In the fifteenth century, however, a new social problem was perceived to exist in Spain. The trouble began in the early summer of 1391, apparently as a result of inflammatory preaching during the Lenten and Passion season, by an Andalusian priest, Ferrán Martínez, archdeacon of Ecija. The preaching took place in Seville, and incited a crowd of local Christians to attack the large and still quite flourishing Jewish community of this port on the Guadalquivir river, the largest and most prosperous city in the region. A rash of similar attacks then spread across the Peninsula, from the south-west to Catalonia in the north-east. The traditionally quoted figures for Jews who died as a result of the 1391 violence seem greatly exaggerated in the cases, for example, of Seville, where 4,000 are said to have been killed, and Córdoba, where 2,000 supposedly died. The figures for Catalan lands, such as 100–250 in Valencia, 250 to 400 in Barcelona, and 78 in Lerida, seem, on the face of it, more plausible. It has to be borne in mind, however, that all these numbers are subjective estimates by contemporary writers and have no reputable documentary basis. In reality, it seems that robbery was a major motive of the violence. This was certainly so in Córdoba, where, somewhat belatedly, Henry III sent in officials to investigate and to secure compensation for his Jewish protégés.[24] The main results of the 1391 pogroms were, firstly, a relatively small amount of death and injury; secondly, considerable loss of property; thirdly, the effective abandonment of the large, traditional Jewish communities in the major cities and migration to smaller towns and villages in the countryside; and finally, and crucially for the future history of Spanish Jewry, large-scale conversion of urban Jews to Christianity. The problem is to track such movements and discover the numbers involved. Ladero has stated that, if the supposition is made that Jews did more or less follow the demographic trends of the rest of the population, it is likely that, after 1400, there were about 75,000 unbaptized Jews in Castile, while 100,000 were baptized between 1391 and about 1410. These figures should be compared with an estimated total population of two-and-a-quarter million in the Crown of Castile. The figures in the Crown of Aragon would be, in each case, about a quarter of the Castilian numbers. In addition, because of the disintegration, partly through conversion and partly through migration, of the larger urban communities such as those of Seville, Córdoba, Toledo, Barcelona, and Valencia, there were probably more towns with Jewish inhabitants in fifteenth-century Spain than there had been before. The overall number of unbaptized Jews though, was considerably smaller and while the remaining Jews tended to move to small towns and villages, the new converts generally stayed in the cities.[25] There is clear evidence of these phenomena in tax records, and it is especially noticeable, in a variety of documentary sources, that, as already noted, Jews found themselves in agrarian activities, perhaps on a larger scale than before.[26]

The most important long-term consequence of the 1391 pogroms, however, was that the weight of religious, social, economic, and political dislike and opposition which had previously been concentrated on the Jews became transferred to the *conversos*, that is, the converts from Judaism to Christianity. In the words of Angus MacKay, 'conversion, which seemed temporarily to solve many tensions, opened more opportunities to the converted Jew, in terms of finance, tax administration and officeholding'.[27] In both Castile and Aragon, the violence of 1391 was followed by Christian missionary pressure, in which the Catalan Dominican friar, Vincent Ferrer, played a leading part. The preaching, including dramatic night-time rallies, and the formal theological disputation held in the Aragonese town of Tortosa in 1413–14 under the auspices of the anti-pope Benedict XIII, in which the Jewish participants appeared to many of their co-religionaries to have put up a poor show, seem to have induced at least as many conversions as had been achieved by the attacks themselves. As Roger Highfield points out, 'for about half a century, it looked as though the *conversos* might indeed be assimilated into Castilian society'.[28] Under the rule of John II of Castile and his contemporaries in Aragon, there was a long and distinguished procession of *converso* administrators and bishops such as the *relator*, or reporter, of the Castilian royal council, Fernán Díaz de Toledo, and bishops Pablo de Santa María, Alonso de Cartagena, Juan Ortega de Maluenda and Gonzalo García de Santa María. In 1449, however, things began to go wrong. There were many political and economic difficulties, particularly in Castile. When the city of Toledo rebelled against the king, in part as a protest against his leading supporter at the time, the constable of Castile, Don Alvaro de Luna, one effect was an attack on the local *conversos*, and an attempt to exclude them from public life on the grounds that they had failed to make a full conversion from their previous religion and behaviour, and therefore constituted a threat to society. Although the rebellion was soon crushed, the issue of the sincerity of the 'New Christians' continued to inspire a lively polemic, during which it was proposed by some that an inquisition was the only method adequate to test their religious orthodoxy. John II's son, Henry IV, made a half-hearted attempt in 1459–60 to introduce the tribunal to Castile, where it had not previously existed. In Aragon, on the other hand, a semi-moribund papal tribunal survived from the period of Cathar influence in the thirteenth and early fourteenth centuries. However, it took social disturbances, political turmoil, and economic difficulties, as well as the determination of the new sovereigns after 1474, Ferdinand and Isabella, to extract the bull founding the new Spanish Inquisition from Sixtus IV in 1478.

The activity of the expanding network of tribunals in both Castile and Aragon – for the Holy Office, unlike all other Spanish institutions, was able to leap over internal frontiers – soon revealed what appeared to be a continuing adherence to Jewish belief and practice on the part of hundreds of converts. This fact, whatever may be thought of the veracity of Inquisition records, seems clearly to have been in the mind of the Catholic Monarchs, as the Borja (alias Borgia) pope Alexander VI was soon to style them, when, in the 1492 expulsion pragmatic, they said that the cause of the Inquisition's problem with the *conversos* was, at least in part, 'the communication of the Jews with the Christians'.[29] The expulsion seems to have been the culmination of a long-standing anxiety on the part of the Church to give converts a chance to become fully integrated into Catholic life.

Although the Castilian and Aragonese Jewish communities had lost many of their members to Christianity as a result of the 1391 pogroms and the subsequent ecclesiastical and legislative pressures, it had always proved an uphill struggle to organize and maintain ghettos in Spanish towns. It is not surprising, therefore, that *conversos* should have been able, when there was good will on both sides as there generally seems to have been, to maintain such close links with unbaptized Jews. As a part of their policy of keeping or restoring order in town and countryside (and it is important always to remember that government measures concerning Jews and *conversos* have to be seen in the context of all their other aims and methods) Ferdinand and Isabella began – in Cáceres in 1478 and confirmed at the Cortes, or parliament in Toledo in 1480 – a policy of returning Jews and Muslims to their respective ghettos, all over Castile. Royal representatives were required to initiate such measures in their districts, and similar measures were attempted in Aragon as well. At the same time, the enforcement of the yellow badge was implemented, and measures were passed to restrict the activities of Jewish moneylenders.[30] Royal policy towards the Jews in the 1480s developed distinctly schizoid tendencies. Though these oppressive laws were being passed with increasing frequency, there is an equal number of orders in the royal archives of Castile which attempted to protect the rights and economic life of the kingdom's Jewish communities. The last recorded measure of this kind was the order to the *corregidor* of Cáceres, in Extremadura, to free some Jews who had been arrested for refusing to pay taxes which had been levied on the Christian population to finance the war to reconquer Granada from the Muslims. This document was issued on 18 January 1492.[31] Just over two months later, the expulsion order was promulgated. In the meantime, though, partial expulsions of Jews had already been implemented. Although in 1480 the right of Jews to take part in the supplying of food to Seville had been reinforced by the Crown, in

1483 Jews were expelled from the whole region of Andalusia then under Christian control, including Seville, though taxation evidence suggests that some were still in Córdoba in 1485.[32] Other, more local, expulsions were also attempted. In 1486, for example, the Jews of Teruel, after being exploited for their testimony by the Inquisition, were ordered to be expelled from the diocese of Albarracín, which covered that town.[33]

Although there was obviously considerable confusion in government circles in the 1480s, concerning policy towards unbaptized Jews, and the continuing links between Jews and *conversos* were certainly worrying both Church and secular authorities, it is still not possible to explain why the expulsion decree was issued in March 1492. Until that date, Ferdinand and Isabella had continued with the policy traditionally followed by all medieval monarchs. The Jews were regarded as royal protégés, they were heavily taxed, and their social life was subject to external regulation, but they were still allowed restricted social, and fuller religious, freedom. The question of their being expelled did not arise. Looking back with hindsight, it is possible to show that pressures of a traditional kind, attacks on moneylending, the imposition of the badge, and atrocity stories, were building up during the fifteenth century, particularly in the 1480s. However, despite the plethora of documentation in the central Castilian and Aragonese archives, the dynamics of political decision-making at the highest level – and it is evident that the expulsion order was just this kind of decision – are poorly understood. Although medieval monarchs such as Ferdinand and Isabella had considerable autocratic power, they were, of course, like all personal rulers, susceptible not only to their own individual idiosyncrasies, but also to lobbying, both through the constitutional process and in less regular and identifiable ways. In late medieval Castile administrative law, produced by the bureaucrats of the central government and the Royal Council, which consisted by this time mainly of legally-trained churchmen and lay civil servants many of them of Jewish origin, had much higher status than parliamentary legislation. In fact, the Catholic Monarchs did not summon their parliaments at all during the Granada war and managed none the less to finance and prosecute a series of extremely expensive campaigns. A similar policy was being attempted, with less success, in Aragon. The vital point, however, is that it was in these administrative circles surrounding the sovereigns that the decision to expel the Jews was taken, just after they, along with other Spaniards, had been publicly celebrating the conquest of Granada and the end of Muslim rule in the Peninsula. Despite the obscurities of the political process, however, it is clear that the most powerful lobby in the case of the expulsion was the Inquisition. Large sections of the 1492 decree itself are simply copied from a memorandum which the Holy Office had supplied to the Crown a few days before. The number of atrocity stories about Spanish Jews, such as the stoning of crosses and ritual murders, increased in the 1480s. It looks as though a publicity campaign was being mounted by the Inquisition, because of the continued links between Jews and *conversos*, in order to discredit Jews in the eyes of the Christian population and thus force the monarchs' hands, just as had been done with the *conversos* when the Inquisition itself had been introduced in 1478. This time, though, the matter was entirely internal to Spain. The Pope need not be involved, thus saving considerably in time and the costs of lobbying.

The methods used to manipulate public opinion are even more obscure than the mechanics of government decision-making, but the Inquisition's meticulous bureaucratic technique does make it possible to see high-pressure lobbying in action in the notorious ritual murder case of the so-called 'Holy Child of La Guardia'. After a consecrated host, or piece of unleavened communion bread, was found in the luggage of a *converso* pilgrim returning home to New Castile from the shrine of St James at Compostela, a child was said to have been lost in Toledo, and a group of Jews and *conversos* was accused of having ritually murdered him at La Guardia. The succeeding trials, in the tribunal at Avila, were, even by the somewhat dubious standards of Inquisition legal practice, a shambles. First, and quite illegally, the Holy Office tried the accused Jews itself. Then the witnesses' testimony could not be harmonized, even after they had been tortured, which was still a rare event at this time, and they were allowed to meet, which was never normally allowed. No parents who had lost a child were ever produced and there was not even a body! None the less, several of the accused were eventually burnt in November 1491, and the case served its purpose. It is known that the Inquisition had the details circulated to all its regional tribunals. This was done as much for the benefit of higher political circles as to edify the general public. The expulsion order very soon followed.[34]

The hard, but vital, question is how many of Spain's Jews refused to convert and preferred to leave after selling their property, for which somewhat optimistic arrangements were made in the royal edict. Once again, there is an acute shortage of reliable figures. The Andalusian Old Christian parish priest, Andrés Bernáldez, estimated 100,000 emigrants, the German traveller, Münzer, agreed, while Abravanel claimed that 300,000 had departed. Modern scholars have scattered their estimates around the figure of 200,000, which looks uncommonly like splitting the difference, but Ladero, in 1975, guessed on the basis of general demographic trends – it is impossible to do more – that between 1400 and 1490 the Jewish population of Spain doubled to 200,000, three-quarters of them living in Castile and the rest in Aragon. He estimated that two-thirds of the Castilian Jews emigrated, the rest staying to convert.[35] However, to obtain a more realistic picture of what happened to Spanish Jewry, it is necessary to go back to 1391, when, despite the depredations of civil war and the Black Death, there were still over 200,000 Jews in the country. It seems probable that more than half the Jews who survived the 1391 pogroms converted afterwards. If their numbers doubled too, in the fifteenth century, then alongside the 200,000 Jews there were at least 300,000 *conversos* in the 1480s. This would suggest that only about a quarter, at most, of the Spaniards of Jewish origin who were living there in the 1480s emigrated in order to remain Jews after 1492.[36]

None the less, whatever may be done to reduce the high traditional estimates of Jewish emigration from Spain, there is no doubt that a major movement of population took place, involving well over 100,000 people, in the four months of the official expulsion period and soon afterwards. Many Jews headed south to the straits of Gibraltar, hoping, in the words of the Andalusian parish priest and chronicler, Andrés Bernáldez, that, just as with a strong hand and outstretched arm, and much honour and riches, God through Moses had miraculously taken the other people of Israel from Egypt, so in these parts of Spain [Andalusia] they had to return [after the earlier 1483, local expulsion] and go out with much honour and riches, without losing any of their goods, to possess the holy promised land, which they confessed to have lost through their great and abominable sins which their ancestors had committed against God.[37]

Bernáldez stresses that such beliefs were held by 'both simple and educated' and goes on to report gleefully that the waters of the Mediterranean did not part for the Jews to cross, and that many of them were attacked and even killed by Muslims when they arrived in the North African kingdoms. None the less, Spanish Jewish communities were established at this time in North Africa which have endured up to the twentieth century. Muslim territory in the eastern Mediterranean also had some attraction for Spanish Jewish émigrés, as will become clear in later chapters. However, there were also possibilities in other Christian lands. Paradoxically, there was still freedom for Jews to settle in papal territories, such as those around Avignon and Vienne, on the east bank of the Rhône, in the papal states in Italy, and even in Rome itself. In 1528, just after the sack of Rome by Imperial troops, a Spanish priest, called Francisco Delicado, whose works include a book on the treatment of syphilis using *guyaco* wood from the Indies, published in Venice a novel about an Andalusian Jewish girl, known as *La lozana andaluza* ('The lusty Andalusian girl'). The heroine was born in Córdoba, into what soon became a broken home, and after many vicissitudes joined a partly-Jewish, partly-*converso* community in Rome, living from earnings as a prostitute, as well as acting as a make-up consultant.[38]

However, by far the largest number of emigrants went to the neighbouring kingdom of Portugal, where freedom of Jewish worship lasted until 1497. There is no doubt that the Spaniards had a major impact on Portuguese Jewish life. Before 1492, the social and economic profile of the ten larger, and the two dozen smaller, communities seems to have corresponded quite closely to that of Spain. Indeed, there had been a previous influx of immigrants from the neighbouring kingdom of Castile during the upheaval which followed the Spanish pogroms of 1391. With the help of somewhat fragmentary taxation evidence, María José Pimenta Ferro Tavares has guessed that there may have been about 30,000 Jews in Portugal in the mid to late fifteenth century, constituting approximately 3 per cent of the total population. Naturally, the largest communities, in Lisbon, Evora, Santarem, and Oporto, had the most elaborate occupational structures. Between 1383 and 1450, no fewer than thirty-eight Jewish occupations are identifiable in Lisbon, while the figures for the same period elsewhere are twenty-two in Evora, nineteen in Santarem, and fourteen in Oporto. It is clear from these and other sources that Portuguese Jews not only played an important role in such conventional activities as tax-farming and administration, medicine, the clothing trade, and other artisanal occupations, but they also held and worked land on a significant scale. Clearly, as in Spain, such agricultural work was more a feature of the smaller towns, and it appears that Jews generally concentrated on 'commercial' products, which might be marketed at some distance from the area of production, such as olive oil and wine, rather than on cereals.[39] This pattern is strikingly similar to that which became increasingly common among Christian landlords in south-western Spain as well as Portugal in the fourteenth and fifteenth centuries. The demographic impact of emigration from Spain in 1492 was very great. It seems likely that the Portuguese Jewish population more or less trebled, to about 10 per cent of the total. Not all the Jews who came initially to Portugal attempted to settle permanently, however. There is much evidence, for example in Inquisition records of the late fifteenth and early sixteenth centuries, that many Spanish Jews quickly returned to Spain and were baptized, though it was hard for them to regain the property which they had disposed of for derisory prices in the expulsion period. In addition, they ran a considerable risk of denunciation to the Holy Office, further property confiscation, and even death. Also, the Portuguese royal council initially allowed Jews to pass through the country, though they extracted 6,000 *cruzados* each from the 600 richest emigrant families in the hope that they would continue to enrich the royal coffers and the rest of the economy. Many of the Spanish immigrants had a hard life, however, living in poverty, or even slavery. John II of Portugal, clearly influenced by religious as well as economic considerations, took many of the children of the less privileged away from their parents, sending them to the new settlement of Santo Tomé in Africa, where it was hoped they would begin an entirely new life as Christians. As early as 1494, moves were made with a view to expelling unbaptized Jews from Portugal, but it was only when John II died and was succeeded by Manuel I that the matter became serious. Faced with the prospect of losing his chance of marrying Princess Isabella, daughter of the Catholic Monarchs, if he did not follow their example in his Jewish policies, the new king ordered an expulsion of all those who refused to convert, to be carried out between December 1496 and the end of October 1497. It seems fairly clear that a mixture of Manuel's own political advantage, the economic interests, both of the Crown and of the country as a whole, and the Church's wish to gain new converts were all involved in the decision to expel. It seems very likely that the king expected most of the Jews to convert, and it is clear that converts were given every encouragement to remain in the country with their assets, given that, in contrast to the situation in Spain, they were to be given ample time to make an adjustment to the new religion, being exempted from any kind of official enquiry into their spiritual life for twenty years. Motives seem to have been genuinely mixed, but one indisputable fact is that there was no Inquisition awaiting those who converted.[40]

This did not mean, though, that atrocities did not occur. The Portuguese chronicler, Damião de Góis, reports that, when a further attempt was made, in 1497, to remove Jewish children under fourteen from parents who refused to convert, so that they might be brought up as Christians, 'many of them killed their children, suffocating them and throwing them into wells and rivers'.[41] As this Christian source indicates, there was, in some respects, more violence in the Portuguese than in the Spanish expulsion, but it is probable that an even higher proportion of Jews remained in Spain, either through self-interest or as a result of political and economic pressure. The development of a 'New Christian' population in Portugal, as much as in Spain, was to have a significant effect on the economic life of western Europe in the sixteenth and seventeenth centuries.

Notes

1 Jonathan Israel, *European Jewry in the Age of Mercantilism, 1550–1750*, Oxford, Clarendon Press, 1985, pp. 5–9.
2 *'The Jews' in St John's Gospel*, London, Centre for Biblical and Jewish Studies, Bulletin 2 (1964).
3 See, for example, John Gager, *The Origins of Anti-Semitism*, New York, Oxford University Press, 1983.
4 Roger Collins, *Early Medieval Spain, Unity in Diversity, 400–1000*, London, Macmillan, 1983, pp. 129–42.
5 *Chronicle of Solomon Bar Simson* in Shlomo Eidelberg, trans. and ed, *The Jews and the Crusaders. The Hebrew Chronicles of the First and Second Crusades*, Madison, Wisconsin University Press, 1977, p. 47. The scriptural quotations are from Psalm 83, vv. 13, 5.
6 Lionel Kochan, *The Jew and his History*, London, Macmillan, 1977, p. 19.
7 Eidelberg, *Jews and the Crusaders*.
8 Jonathan Riley-Smith, *The First Crusade and the Idea of Crusading*, London, Athlone Press, 1986, p. 53.
9 The relevant Church legislation is surveyed, with texts, in Solomon Grayzel, *The Church and the Jews in the Thirteenth Century*, Philadelphia, Jewish Publication Society of America, 1933.
10 Jeremy Cohen, *The Friars and the Jews: the Evolution of Medieval Anti-Judaism*, Ithaca and London, Cornell University Press, 1982.
11 A lively general survey in Norman Cohn, *The pursuit of the Millennium: Revolutionary Millenarians and Mystical Anarchists of the Middle Ages*, London, Secker & Warburg, 1957.
12 Riley-Smith, *First Crusade*, pp. 33–5, 142–3.
13 Hyam Maccoby, ed. and trans., *Judaism on Trial. Jewish-Christian Disputations in the Middle Ages*, London and Toronto, Associated University Presses, 1982, has texts and introduction.
14 For a thirteenth-century English case, see F. D. Logan, 'Thirteen London Jews and conversion to Christianity: problems of apostasy in the 1280s', *Bulletin of the Institute of Historical Research*, xlv (1972), pp. 214–29.
15 Text in Grayzel, *The Church*, p. 241 n. 96 and Maccoby, *Judaism*, pp. 21–2.
16 Cohen, *The Friars*, pp. 52–60.
17 Nicholas Eymerich, *Le Manuel des Inquisiteurs*, ed and trans. by L. Sala-Molins, Paris, Mouton, 1973, pp. 75–80.
18 Bernhard Blumenkranz, *Le juif médiéval au miroir de l'art chrétien*, Paris, Etudes Augustiniennes, 1966.
19 Joshua Trachtenberg, *The Devil and the Jews*, New Haven, Yale University Press, 1943.
20 Thérèse and Mendel Metzger, *Jewish Life in the Middle Ages. Illuminated*

Hebrew Manuscripts of the Thirteenth to the Sixteenth Centuries, New York, Alpine Fine Arts Collection, 1982.

21 Malcolm Barber, 'Lepers, Jews and Moslems: the plot to overthrow Christendom in 1321', *History*, lxvi (1981), 1–17.

22 Blumenkranz, *Le juif*, pp. 97–104.

23 Thomas of Monmouth, *The Life and Miracles of St William of Norwich*, eds A. Jessopp and M. R. James, Cambridge, Cambridge University Press, 1896.

24 Michel Mollat and Philippe Wolff, *The Popular Revolutions of the Late Middle Ages*, London, George Allen & Unwin, 1973, pp. 211–25; Wolff, 'The 1391 pogrom in Spain. Social crisis or not?', *Past and Present*, 50 (1971), 4–18; John Edwards, 'Religious belief and social conformity: the *converso* problem in late-medieval Córdoba', *Transactions of the Royal Historical Society*, 5th series, xxxi (1981), 117.

25 Miguel Angel Ladero Quesada, 'Le nombre des juifs dans la Castille du XVe siècle', *Proceedings of the Sixth World Congress of Jewish Studies (Jerusalem, 1975)*, ii. 45–52; Luis Suárez Fernández, *Documentos Acerca de la Expulsión de los Judíos* (Valladolid, 1964), pp. 65–72.

26 See, for example, Francisco Cantera Burgos and Carlos Carrete Parrondo, 'La judería de Hita', *Sefarad*, xxxii (1972), 249–99.

27 Angus MacKay, 'Popular movements and pogroms in fifteenth-century Castile', *Past and Present*, 55 (1972), pp. 45–6.

28 Roger Highfield, 'Christians, Jews and Muslims in the same society: the fall of *convivencia* in medieval Spain', *Studies in Church History*, xv (1977), ed. D. Baker, pp. 125–6.

29 Suárez Fernández, *Documentos*, p. 392.

30 ibid., pp. 140–2, 331–3, 338–40, 194–5.

31 ibid., pp. 387–8.

32 ibid., p. 164; Edwards, 'Religious belief', 117.

33 The Jews were still in Teruel, however, in 1492. Fritz (Yitzhak) Baer, *Die Juden im Christlichen Spanien*, 2 vols, Berlin 1929–33, repr. Farnborough, 1970, i, p. 569; Henry Kamen, 'The Mediterranean and the expulsion of Spanish Jews in 1492', *Past and Present*, 119 (1988), 52–3n.

34 Maurice Kriegel, 'La prise d'une décision: l'expulsion des Juifs d'Espagne en 1492', *Révue Historique*, cclx (1968), 49–90; Fidel Fita, 'La verdad sobre el martirio del Santo Niño de La Guardia, o sea el proceso y quema (16 noviembre 1491) del judío Juce Franco en Avila', *Boletín de la Real Academia de la Historia*, xi (1887), 7–134.

35 Ladero, 'Le nombre', 47.

36 ibid., 46.

37 Andrés Bernáldez, *Memorias del Reinado de los Reyes Católicos*, eds Manuel Gómez-Moreno and Juan de Mata Carriazo, Madrid, CSIC, 1962, p. 254.

38 Francisco Delicado, *La Lozana Andaluza*, ed Bruno Damiani, Madrid, Castalia, 1982.

39 María José Pimenta Ferro Tavares, *Os Judeus em Portugal no Seculo XV*, Lisbon, Universidad Nova, 1982, pp. 22–80, 107–12, 273–85, 303–5.

40 I. S. Révah, 'Les Marranes portugais et l'Inquisition au XVIe siècle', in *The Sephardi Heritage, Essays on the History and Cultural Contribution of the Jews of Spain and Portugal*, i, *The Jews of Spain and Portugal before and after the Expulsion of 1492*, ed Richard D. Barnett, London, Valentine-Mitchell, 1972, pp. 479–526.

41 Damião de Góis, *Crónica do Felicíssimo Rei D. Manuel*, extracts ed Antonio Alvaro Dória, Lisbon, Livraria Clasica Editora, 1944, p. 54.

2
Renaissance, Reformation, and the Jews

In 1500, it would probably have appeared to most Christians in western and central Europe that the great programme of Church reform, which had begun to develop in the eleventh century and which had been systematically set out in the canons of the Fourth Lateran Council of 1215, would continue for the foreseeable future. From the point of view of both ecclesiastical and secular hierarchies, serious upsets and difficulties such as heresy, the Great Schism of the Catholic Church, and warfare between Christian states, which had occurred during the fourteenth and fifteenth centuries, appeared to have been overcome or at least brought under some kind of control. Then, however, according to traditional historiography, new and threatening developments occurred, which were to destroy whatever unity the medieval Church had been able to achieve and retain. In political terms, new and ever more damaging military conflicts broke out, but these were influenced, or even apparently caused, by two primarily intellectual and religious movements, known generally as the Renaissance and the Reformation. The issue raised by such an approach to the sixteenth and seventeenth centuries is that of how far educated thought was capable of being translated, first into public policy and then into action at all levels of society. It is this question which makes it necessary to examine the influence, if any, of the Renaissance and Reformation on the life of Jews in Catholic Europe. It is inevitable, therefore, that this chapter will primarily concern thought rather than practical policy and its results. The latter areas will be examined in succeeding chapters.

In addition, a further point needs to be noted at this stage. In view of the fact that the motive forces behind the Renaissance and Reformation were very much a Christian phenomenon, the perspective of what immediately follows will be largely a Christian view of the Jews, rather than vice versa, though the traffic of ideas, as will become clear, was not wholly in one direction. The influence of Renaissance thought on contemporary Jewish communities is also a matter of some significance.

The Renaissance and the Jews

The concept of 'Renaissance', or 'rebirth' is itself quite controversial, in its definition and hence in its time-scale. If one starts from the basic assumption that it relates originally to a restoration of earlier cultural values, specifically those of ancient Greece and Rome, and that this first happened in Italy in the fourteenth and fifteenth centuries, then it is possible for the term 'Renaissance' to have some utility. The matter has become more complex, however, since the word has also been applied to other, earlier cultural revivals of a classical nature, such as those supposed to have happened in Charlemagne's empire and in the twelfth century. In terms of later history, however, it is the revival and development of classicism in Italy in the fifteenth century which is of particular significance to relations between Christians and Jews, though it will also be necessary to look at some developments elsewhere.

In Spain before the expulsion, there had been cultural and academic contacts between Christians and Jews which led to specific intellectual achievements. It is questionable, however, whether these should be linked specifically to the Renaissance. The matter is still controversial among scholars, particularly where it concerns the concept of humanism, which will be so important in the discussion which follows. It is probably fairly safe to say that humanism, as well as being closely associated with the revival and development of Greek and Roman culture, has religious significance, in that it implies a more exalted understanding than had perhaps been evident earlier of human beings' own potential for happiness and a stable future. Thus it involves a lowering of estimates of the influence of external forces, such as God or natural phenomena, on the conduct of human affairs. If these two aspects of humanism are applied to late medieval Spain, it seems clear that nothing which closely parallels Italian developments seems to happen until the second half of the fifteenth century. A few scholars visited Italy, some wrote in 'humanist' Latin, the chronicler Alfonso de Palencia for example, but recent scholarship suggests that the prevailing character of Spanish humanism before 1500 involved the use of the vernacular languages rather than Latin, and developed in two main ways – to satisfy the historical interests, respectively, of the military aristocracy, and of servants of the Castilian monarchy in particular.[1] Academic links between Jews and Christians in fifteenth-century Spain seem largely to have concerned Biblical scholarship. J. N. Hillgarth quotes the remark made in 1422 by the master of the military order of Calatrava to Rabbi Moses Arragel that, 'in the time we have free from warring on the wicked Moors, we prefer to listen to the Bible rather than going hunting or listening to historical or poetic works or playing chess'.[2] The translation of the Hebrew scriptures which the rabbi duly prepared, not unnaturally with some misgivings, is generally known as the 'Alba Bible'. It is significant not only for being a vernacular translation, the ownership of which became illegal after 1492, but because it included rabbinical commentaries on the text, as well as Jewish-inspired illustrations which particularly stressed the major Jewish feasts, worship in the Temple and contemporary synagogue worship. The phenomenon of Jewish collaboration with Spanish translations of the Bible had some influence, as will be seen, on later developments in Italy, but, although it involved a deliberate flouting of late medieval practice, it was a purely aristocratic interest and apparently had no connection with the Renaissance as such.

Christian Hebraism

The ideas of certain intellectual circles in Italy in the fifteenth and early sixteenth centuries led, perhaps paradoxically to an interest in Judaism and Hebrew matters which in a certain sense paralleled that in Spain, but which took a very different, and more influential, course. As Frances Yates remarked, 'The great forward movements of the Renaissance all derive their vigour, their emotional impulse, from looking backwards. . . . The past was always better than the present, and progress was revival, rebirth, renaissance of antiquity.'[3] In addition to Greece and Rome, the Hebrew language and Judaism became, to those who held such a view, an object of interest and even of admiration and emulation, seeing that late medieval Europe was not pagan but supposedly Christian and that in Jesus's words even in John's gospel, 'Salvation is of the Jews'.[4] Knowledge of, and interest in, the Hebrew language might occur among Christians who had little or no opportunity to meet a living Jew. This happened, for example, in France where a fairly small group of scholars, in Baron's words, pursued 'Hebrew studies principally for the sake of true knowledge', and not in order to achieve practical social results. Before 1520 Francis I imported an Italian bishop, Augustino Giustiniani, to organize 'oriental studies', which included Hebrew, in France. The Collège de France, founded in 1530, offered Hebrew teaching from the start, and the French-speaking Hebraists of the early sixteenth century included Francois Tissard and the Fleming Nicolas Clénart, or Cleynaert. The latter, in a manner similar to that of the Lullian orientalist and missionary school of the early fourteenth century, travelled to the Maghreb, commenting perceptively in 1540 to his friend Bishop Jean Petit, from Fez, that, ' I live here among Jews who have long been more amazed that Christians exist, than we are that there are still some Jews around'.[5] Such enlightenment had, unfortunately, little or no practical result.

The main area in which Renaissance humanists came into contact with Jewish ideas was in the realm of magic, and here by far the most important activities were first in Italy and then in Germany. Before looking at the main developments in more detail, it is important, though, to give some indication of what 'magic' meant in the period, and how scholars attempt to analyse and study it today. Non-rational and non-human factors as causes of events in human life were assumed to be a reality by virtually, if not actually, everyone in the medieval period, and it is here that historiographical problems arise for most modern scholars. They have to deal with a different mental world, in which people had a different sense of time and a surprising lack of concern, even among 'professionals' in trade and government, for statistical precision. It is rare, for example, to find a medieval account correctly added up, even with the help of an abacus. The cosmology of the time is, however, the most relevant feature here. Medieval people believed themselves to live in a world which was placed in the midst between heaven and hell, and surrounded by invisible beings or spirits. More educated people elaborated a notion of hierarchy among these spirits. Those influenced by the official teachings of Christianity or Judaism attempted to incorporate their cosmology into their religion, or vice versa, nevertheless it would be right to assume, that in their willingness to accept the reality of 'spirits', there was no great difference of mentality between the learned scholar or religious leader and the most humble peasant or artisan. If this is borne in mind, the activities of the Christian Hebraists may be more readily comprehensible.[6]

There was a hierarchy, in late medieval and Renaissance perceptions of magic, to match that which was believed to exist in the spirit world. In order to understand this, it is necessary also to include the question of witchcraft. Organized religion attempted to control and use the spiritual forces of the world for its own purposes, in the Christian case through sacramental activity, such as prayers for people and crops, and, using the term in a less general and more technical sense, in healing with prayer and holy oil and the exorcizing of spirits. Such activity was, however, addressing a deep-rooted human problem which existed long before the arrival of Christianity. This was the problem of evil; the fact that things go wrong in the world and damage or end people's lives. In late medieval Europe and on into the sixteenth and seventeenth centuries, the priests and laymen, who attempted to harness the power given to them by God as part of the hierarchy of the Church in order to improve the lot of their fellow-Christians and of themselves, often found themselves working alongside 'unofficial' practitioners, who were attempting to perform the same task. What was going on may be termed 'white magic', that is the harnessing of occult forces for good purposes. Europe was therefore full of healers and sorcerers who deployed an enormous and varied battery of spells, charms, prayers, and tokens, in order to do good to others. There remained the possibility, however, that if such forces, whether within or outside the Church, were indeed effective, they might equally well be used for evil purposes. Thus sacred objects with healing power, such as holy oil or the consecrated bread of the Mass which was commonly retained for later use, would be guarded and locked up, so that they might not fall into the wrong hands. There was little or no control, however, over the non-ecclesiastical healers, magicians, or witches, who did so steady a trade in all parts of society. They were largely free to use their skills for good or evil, and, up to the fifteenth century, the Church contained two contradictory traditional attitudes towards 'black magic', or *maleficium*, or witchcraft. Fundamentally, of course, the Church claimed complete power, granted by God through Jesus, over all dealings between humans and spirits, whether for good or bad purposes, and it was therefore in general opposed to all such activity except its own. However, when it came to evil magic, a disagreement arose over the approach to be adopted. On the one hand, the *Canon episcopi*, which had been incorporated into canon law since the twelfth century, rejected all notion of an alternative 'black' or 'witch' religion, like some kind of inverse or negative version of Christianity. By the late fifteenth century, however, an alternative view had developed in which this elaborate witch religion, always significantly involving females, was accepted as a reality, with its ointments, its night journeys to 'sabbats' and its sexual encounters with the Devil. The theory, perhaps best represented by the *Malleus Maleficarum*, or *Hammer of the Witches*, a German Dominican handbook of 1486, was already spilling over into practice, and, in view of the diabolization of both Christian heretics and Jews which had increasingly been occurring in the late Middle Ages, it may not be entirely coincidental that witch-persecutions and expulsions of Jews should have happened on a large scale at about the same time.

D. P. Walker provided a useful analytical method by distinguishing between subjective magic, in which the practitioner alone is involved, and transitive magic, in which he or she attempts to produce an effect in or on another person, but not on the individual carrying out the magic. As he notes, 'it is only transitive operations that can be socially important'. There is, however, another important principle which must also be borne in mind. This is the notion that,

> A formula of words . . . may not only be an adequate substitute for the things denoted, but may even be more powerful. Instead of collecting together groups of planetary objects [as in astrology], we can, by naming them correctly by their real, ancient names, obtain an even greater celestial force.[7]

It is precisely in this activity that some Christian students and practitioners of white magic turned to the Jews and found that they had to attempt to become Hebraists. They were fascinated by an older, Jewish mystical tradition known generally as Kabbalah in Jewish writing, though often usefully distinguished as 'Cabala' or 'Cabbala' when found in a Christian context. There are two main facets in Kabbalah, as it first developed in the south of France and in Spain in the twelfth and thirteenth centuries and as it was known in the fifteenth and sixteenth centuries. It is important always to bear in mind that Kabbalah is primarily a method of coming to know God better. It is thus, when properly understood, an integral part of orthodox Judaism. The first basic Kabbalistic doctrine is that the Godhead may be understood as having ten particular attributes, known as *sefirot*, which are, in Scholem's words, 'the ten names most common to God and in their entirety they form his one great Name', which in Hebrew thought means the same as God Himself. The *sefirot* are thus 'the creative names which God called into the world'.[8] They conventionally represent 'crown', 'understanding', 'wisdom', 'power', 'love' or 'mercy', 'heaven' or the 'sun', 'beauty', 'majesty', 'endurance', 'foundation' or 'covenant', and, finally, a principle known as '*shekinah*', or 'presence'. Each of these attributes of God attracted several meanings and explanations in Kabbalistic writings, and the *shekinah* acquired the characteristics of the feminine side of God. The second main feature of Kabbalah is the use which it makes of the twenty-two letters of the Hebrew alphabet. According to the Spanish tradition, this alphabet contains the Name or Names of God, so that, when the Kabbalist studies the Scriptures, and in particular the book of Genesis, he is contemplating both God Himself and also the works God does through the power of His name. Thus two main traditions developed in Spanish Kabbalism, one based on the *sefirot* and the other on the letters of the alphabet. Kabbalah became what D. P. Walker calls 'transitive' and Frances Yates 'operative' magic. Involved in this activity was another technique, known as *gematria*, in which calculations were done with the numerical equivalents which all Hebrew letters conventionally possess.

The attraction of Kabbalah to Christian scholars seems to have been the opportunities which it offered to those who wished to improve their understanding of God to approach Him more nearly, and to help bring the world into greater accordance with His will. The earliest important Christian Cabalist was Marsilio Ficino (1433–99), a Florentine, who, in his *Of the Christian religion*, published in 1474, both showed an awareness of the Talmud and of rabbinical interpretations of Scripture and used Kabbalistic material. Opinions still seem to divide, on Jewish and non-Jewish lines, when it comes to the next major figure in Renaissance magic and Christian Cabalism, Giovanni Pico della Mirandola, a younger contemporary of Ficino. Pico was interested in the practical side of Cabala, that is, the attempt to harness spiritual powers in order to change reality. Frances Yates thought Pico knew Hebrew 'quite well, or at least much better than any Gentile contemporary'.[9] Baron, on the other hand, has a low opinion of Pico's professionalism, quoting the words of Haim Wirzubski on the Renaissance scholar's sermon about Jesus's passion, or last days. Pico, Wirzubski said, was

> aware of what his distinguished audience would gladly listen to, as well as of their ignorance of the Hebrew language and of Jewish sources. Secure in that awareness, he went on for two hours to impress them with a show of derivative erudition in his long-winded sermon, the highlights of which are as often as not sham revelations from made-up authorities.[10]

There is certainly good reason to doubt both Pico's linguistic competence and his understanding of the place of Kabbalah within Judaism. He seems to have equated it with the oral law, which in reality was normally understood to be the Talmud. In addition, it is clear, from the work of Frances Yates, that Judaism was far from being the only source of Pico's ideas on magic. He was also involved in the use of certain mystical texts of the second to third centuries C.E. which were mistakenly attributed, in the Renaissance period, to Hermes Trismegistus, or 'Thrice-great'. He was one of the five incarnations of the Greek god Hermes, the Roman Mercury, who was also, somewhat remarkably, identified with the Egyptian god Thoth. The so-called Hermetic writings had a considerable vogue in the Renaissance period, and were often regarded by Christians as another version of the 'oral law', supposedly given to Moses on Sinai, together with the Cabala. They will appear again, in a context very different from that of fifteenth-century Italy.

There are two main questions which arise in relation to Christian Cabalism. The first is the attitude of the scholars to the Jewish texts which they studied, often with Jewish help, if even then imperfectly; and the second is the influence which this Jewish–Christian contact, however limited, may have had on the adherents of the two religions. From their very different points of view, Yates and Baron are agreed that Pico's interest in Kabbalah had little or nothing to do with acquiring a better understanding of Judaism. On one occasion he stated, 'No science can be more efficacious in demonstrating the divinity of Christ than magic and cabala.' His seventh *Conclusion*, one of seventy-two which were claimed to have come straight from the Jewish texts, stated that 'No Hebrew Kabbalist can deny that the name of Jesus, if we interpret it according to Kabbalistic principles and methods, signifies God, the Son of God, and the Wisdom of the Father through the divinity of the Third Person.' Also typical of Christian Hebraists' attitudes to Kabbalah was the title given by the French humanist Guillaume Postel to his unpublished Latin translation of the *Zohar*, the best-known Spanish Kabbalistic text:

The work of oral law, or the harmonisation of nature and grace restored to unity. It is named the Zohar, or the supreme splendour and is the product of that Simon the Just, the last high priest of the Jews, who had taken Christ into his arms. . . . Its subject matter is the truth of the Gospel and of the correct interpretation handed down in most secret commentaries from Moses to Christ under the guidance of the inscrutable judgement of the Holy Spirit, as confirmed by Christ through good deeds and doctrines.[11]

So many of the yearnings for a golden age and for religious unity, which were to be deeply felt in the early modern period, are contained in these sentences. However, despite the obvious gap between Christian and Jewish views of Kabbalah, it would be wrong to suppose that scholars of the two religions did not influence one another. As Moshe Idel has pointed out, one remarkable feature of the Renaissance period in Italy was that, unlike in earlier centuries such as the time of Maimonides when the traffic in ideas was almost entirely into Judaism from outside, on this occasion the Christians (and in particular Florentine Neo-Platonists such as Ficino and Pico) sought ideas from the Jews. Idel stresses the subdivision in Kabbalah between the Spanish and Italian traditions, the latter showing less interest in the attempt to use orthodox Judaism as the only Kabbalistic context. Christians were, for example, attracted by the work of the Spaniard, Abraham Abulafia, which, though done in the thirteenth century was popular in some circles in fifteenth-century Italy. In Scholem's view, Abulafia used Kabbalah subjectively, on himself, as, in Frances Yates's words, 'a kind of self-hypnosis'. The attractiveness of such a technique to Christians was that it did not depend on any one theological system and could therefore easily be incorporated into the mixture of pagan, Christian, and 'hermetic' sources which formed the basis of much Renaissance philosophical and religious thought. Now some Jews, such as Yohanan Alemanno, Isaac and Judah Abravanel, Judah Moscato, and Abraham Yagel, began to follow the example of their Christian colleagues. Magic thus became 'respectable' in at least some Jewish circles, though Idel argues that its influence in its Italian form was never great, and was soon eclipsed by the development of the Spanish Kabbalah in Safed in Palestine.[12]

Reuchlin and German Hebraism

There had always been some interest in Hebrew and Judaism in medieval Europe, including the Empire, but in the fifteenth century humanistic ideas gradually began to influence some scholars' approaches to the subject. The intellectual and social atmosphere (being of course closely connected) were not at all the same in Germany and Italy. It is clear that the Italian humanists were not particularly interested in understanding Judaism for its own sake, but rather sought more ammunition partly from Jewish biblical work but mainly from Kabbalah, to bolster their existing religious convictions. Nevertheless they seem, with a few exceptions, to have had little interest in religious polemic. In Germany, on the other hand, the situation was more tense and the religious climate more heated and hostile to Judaism. The connection with the large-scale expulsions of communities taking place at the time the German Renaissance Hebraists were working cannot be ignored and will be considered in due course, but there are also two other special features of the German situation which have caused it to be viewed in a very different perspective from Italy. The first of these is the fact that the major Christian reform movement which has come to be known as the Reformation happened in the same period as the German Renaissance, so that Christian theology became the major issue in much of intellectual life; in addition, social and political upheaval, far greater than that in the Italian Church, inevitably coloured German scholars' attitude to Judaism and the Jews. The second special feature is a historiographical one which must be faced by anyone writing, in the late twentieth century, about Christians and Jews, especially in Germany. In Heiko Oberman's wise words, 'We are writing history in the wake of the Nazi massacres. . . . We are still so haunted by a nightmare which continues to be a daily reality, that in our field it is hard to find a middle ground between aggressive accusations and escapist apologies.'[13] Perhaps this statement is truer of some theologians than of much of the historical profession, which still largely ignores the Jews. There is, none the less, a real problem here, which will become obvious, not only in the discussion of the views of Johannes Reuchlin and the German Hebraists but also in the consideration of the attitudes of Erasmus and the leading Christian reformers themselves to Judaism and the Jews. Hostile statements by Renaissance and Reformation figures are very likely to seem even more terrible today, against the backcloth of

Auschwitz, than when they were originally delivered. Thoughts about the role which these sixteenth-century figures may have played in creating the conditions for the Holocaust are inevitable, but this fact makes it even more important to attempt also to study them in their own historical context, to relate them to their own immediate circumstances.

Before the importance of Luther became clear to his contemporaries, there was already a controversy raging in German academic and theological circles over the views and activities of Reuchlin. He seems to have been thoroughly at home in the Hebrew language, unlike his contemporary Erasmus, who in 1504 told John Colet, Dean of St Paul's, that he had had to give it up because of pressure of work. The trouble took a while to develop. Reuchlin was born in 1483, but was already establishing himself as a Hebrew scholar when in 1509 Johannes Pfefferkorn, a converted Jew, obtained a commission from Emperor Maximilian to confiscate Jewish books throughout the Empire. This clearly affected Reuchlin, who had dedicated himself to the study of Jewish texts. In 1510, political pressures made the Emperor suspend Pfefferkorn's commission, and, in his frustration, the convert attacked Reuchlin in print in the abusive and personal manner in which intellectual debate was customarily conducted at the time, accusing him of plagiarism and of taking bribes from Jews. After an exchange of pamphlets involving Reuchlin and both Pfefferkorn and the Cologne theologians, the issue turned from 'Judaizing', as Christian jargon had it, to unorthodoxy, when in 1513 Reuchlin was unsuccessfully summonsed to appear before the Dominican inquisitor of Cologne, Jakob von Hochstraten. For the next six years, while controversy raged in Germany, the Dominican attempted to have Reuchlin's views condemned in Rome, but by then a certain Augustinian friar was beginning to cause even greater problems for the Catholic Church.

In order to discover Reuchlin's attitude to Judaism, it is necessary to go back to earlier works, beginning with the *De Verbo Mirifico* ('Of the wonderworking word'), published in Basle in 1494, which Oberman describes as 'a programme to recover the divine gift of the occult sciences which enables man to master the forces of nature by means of the Kabbalah'. The work is in the conventional Classical and Renaissance form of a trialogue, or *sectarum controversia* ('controversy between sects'), between Sidon, a former Epicurean and spokesman for pagan philosophy, Baruch, a learned Jew, and Capnion, a Christian, who speaks for the author. Before Baruch can repent and be baptized, which is the dénouement, he has to renounce the Talmud, though he is allowed to retain the Hebrew language and the Kabbalah. In Capnion's words,

'You [clearly meaning the whole Jewish people] have subverted the Holy Books, therefore you rattle off your prayers in vain, because you speak to Him in self-made prayers, not in the way God wants to be worshipped. At the same time you hate us, us the true worshippers of God. You hate us with a never-ending hatred.'

Continuing in the conventional medieval anti-Judaic mode, on Good Friday Capnion uses the collect, or prayer, for the 'perfidious Jews', adding,

'I pray to God that he will illumine and convert them to the right faith, so that they are liberated from captivity by the Devil. . . . Once they acknowledge Jesus to be the true Messiah, everything will turn to their good in this world and in the world to come. Amen.'

In 1504, in a *German Open Letter*, Reuchlin clearly stated that he regarded 'the Jews' as collectively guilty of the death of Jesus, which they called upon themselves in the famous statement by the crowd in Matthew's gospel (ch. 27 v. 25), during the trial of Jesus, 'His blood be on us and on our children'. Following conventional medieval Church teaching, Reuchlin believed that the Jews could not repent, because of their blindness, but he did allow one escape route which shows the influence of Renaissance Hebraism. If a Jew was learned, understood here, of course, in humanist vernacular as having a knowledge of the Greek and Roman classics, and engaged in Kabbalistic study which interpreted to him the Names of God (meaning in fact *Jeschuh (sic)*, or Jesus), then he might be saved from his error and join the true faith.

In his book, *The Rudiments of Hebrew*, published in 1506, Reuchlin acknowledged the help he had received in learning the Hebrew alphabet from Jacob Yehiel Loans, Jewish physician to the Emperor Frederick III. But he stated that none the less he had three main enemies in his work, humanists, scholastics, and the Jews. Jews, he said, were unwilling to teach Hebrew to Christians, and therefore he had to work mostly on his own, and advocated that converts from Judaism should be employed to teach the language. Like the thirteenth-century friars, Reuchlin saw the Talmud as a major barrier between Jews and conversion to Christianity. When under pressure during his conflict with Pfefferkorn, because of his Jewish contacts, he stated, in his famous pamphlet the *Augenspiegel* ('Mirror to the eye'), that he would be prepared to see the 'blasphemous' parts of the Talmud confiscated and stored in Christian libraries. In saying this he accepted, whether consciously or not, one of the main theses of Gregory IX's 1236 letter. In his social attitudes, Reuchlin seems to have wanted to continue the 'Augustinian' policy towards Jews in Christian society, allowing them limited freedom in their personal and religious lives, no longer regarding them as 'serfs' or 'slaves' as was conventional in medieval law, but firmly separating them from Christians, in the style of the Fourth Lateran Council. In essence, despite the veneer of Cabalism and humanistic learning, little seems to have changed.

Erasmus

The attitude towards the Reuchlin controversy of the Dutch humanist Erasmus, advocate of the 'philosophy of Christ', is in itself revealing of his approach to Judaism and Jews. He honoured the German Hebraist for his fight for academic freedom against scholastically trained theologians and the Inquisition, but had very little time for his views. Indeed, Erasmus's published comments on Jews and Judaism have a hostility and bitterness in them which are liable to startle those who see him as the advocate of a simple, undogmatic, evangelical Christian faith, an opponent of secular warfare as well as ecclesiastical abuses, and an influence for moderation and tolerance in the increasingly turbulent world of the Reformation. Unconverted

Jews seem to have had little or no place in the benevolent dispensation he proposed. It seems probable that Erasmus's views were formed partly by medieval social prejudice, despite the fact that he is unlikely to have seen a practising Jew in his youth in the Low Countries and Paris, and to a larger extent by his interpretation of Christianity. In a letter to the Paris theological faculty, for example, he seems clearly to transfer Paul's New Testament condemnation of Jewish 'legalism' to the Jews of his own time, when he writes that 'we tolerate an impious and blaspheming people'. Similarly, a phrase in a letter to Wolfgang Capito in 1517, in which Erasmus refers to the possible revival of Judaism which was being discussed in the somewhat fevered Christian theological climate of the time as 'the most pernicious plague', is optimistically interpreted by the humanist's modern editor, Father McConica, as a Pauline reference, but more plausibly by Oberman as containing an element of social prejudice too. There really is too much evidence of such views for it to be possible to sustain the argument that Erasmus did not fully share the anti-Jewish prejudices of his own day. He seems to have believed in Jewish conspiracies, blaming Jews for Pfefferkorn's attack on Reuchlin, and later for the German peasants' war. He wrote that France was 'the most spotless and most flourishing part of Christendom' 'not infected with heretics, with Bohemian schismatics, with Jews, with half-Jewish marranos'. The sixteenth century was to prove the inaccuracy of this observation, but the depth of prejudice beneath it is obvious enough. Even the Hebrew bible was subjected to an attack which went far beyond the conventions of medieval Christianity. In order to prevent the upsurge in Judaism which he seems genuinely to have feared, he was even prepared to abandon the Old Testament all together. 'If only the Church', he wrote, 'would not attach so much importance to the Old Testament – it is a book of shadows, given just for a time'. But then Erasmus would no doubt have condemned the recitation of the psalms, which was the basis of the worshipping life of the Christian monastic orders and secular clergy, as mere 'monkishness'. If such expressions are borne in mind, it may be possible to understand Erasmus's otherwise remarkable attitude to Reuchlin's troubles. It has already been noted that the Netherlander regarded the German as defensible on the grounds of academic freedom, but this did not mean approval of Hebraic studies. Indeed, although Erasmus stated that Reuchlin was 'a second Jerome', comparing his skills in Greek, Latin, and Hebrew with those of the translator to whom the Latin Vulgate Bible was traditionally attributed, this could scarcely be seen as a compliment from one whose own Greek New Testament was to expose, by means of humanistic critical principles, the erroneous nature of much of Jerome's work. The point becomes unambiguous in Erasmus's statement that Hebraism was a blot on Reuchlin, and that his Jewish helpers were doing to him what Satan had once done to the Scribes and Pharisees, that is, blinding him to the truth of the Gospel. It does begin to seem that the Netherlander took to heart his failure to master Hebrew, and the contrast with the attitude of his Italian colleagues could not be more obvious. Once again, it is important to remember that all academic controversy in the Renaissance period used very strong language, but there is none the less good reason to suppose that Erasmus's philosophical and theological convictions naturally led to hostility towards Jewish modes of thought. Dualism between body and spirit, with a strong emphasis on the intrinsic wickedness of the former and the goodness, or potential goodness, of the latter, is discernible in the New Testament, and particularly in Erasmus's favourite writer, Paul. This bias towards the spiritual and against the material could only have been strengthened by the Netherlander's philosophical studies. When combined with the conventional anti-Jewish social prejudices of his contemporaries, Erasmus's personal version of the Christian faith, which appealed to certain academic and political circles in various parts of Europe, could make a dangerous mixture. Practical policy towards Jews was, however, the activity of others.[14]

Luther

Nowhere more than in the assessment of the attitude towards the Jews of the central figure of the earlier Reformation, Martin Luther, do the events of 1933–45 threaten to affect historical study of the sixteenth century. Ever since the end of the Third Reich, and particularly in the period surrounding the 500th anniversary of

Luther's birth in 1983, efforts have been made by historians and theologians to trace the links between the Lutheran Reformation and the attitude of the bulk of Lutheranism to the policy of the Nazis towards the Jews. Luther's own major utterances concerning the Jews, in systematic treatises, letters, and reported 'table-talk', have been endlessly sifted, analysed, and explicitly linked both to Nazi policy and to the attitudes of twentieth-century theologians, including Dietrich Bonhoeffer.[15] Such work needs to be approached with caution by the social historian. It has to be borne in mind that the horror of the Holocaust has, since 1945, led to much theological self-searching, among both Christians and Jews. Although attitudes vary considerably within the two religions, the words of the Anglican priest Alan Ecclestone are typical of much of the resulting thought: 'The shadow cast by the rejection of Judaism carried to such lengths both by the Christian Church and by the secular state falls across our world.'[16]

The liberal rabbi Dow Marmur regards Jewish attempts at conciliation of anti-Semites, whether by assimilation or by any other method, as doomed to failure, though he does look forward to greater self-assertion by Jews in the future.[17] It is, of course, very difficult to avoid allowing the events which have occurred since the sixteenth century to intrude into the consideration of Luther's views on Judaism and the Jews, but it is in any case important to place his statements on the subject in chronological order and attempt to take account of their various contexts.

The conclusion of recent scholars is that no distinction, at the fundamental level, may be made between Luther's earliest recorded views on Judaism and his later, notorious utterances. The reaction of the young friar to the Reuchlin controversy, as early as 1514, was entirely within the medieval Catholic tradition. He was indeed opposed to the burning of Jewish texts, but only because he regarded it as inevitable, as the prophets foretold, that the Jews would curse and blaspheme against Jesus. His argument was truly, and hardly surprisingly, Augustinian. For him, as for the rest of his order, it was obvious, even to the newest student, that to attempt to purge the Jews of blasphemy, in this case by destroying their non-Biblical works, would be to interfere with God's plan. In this way, the thirteenth-century controversy, which Jeremy Cohen describes (see pp. 16–19), lived on in a very

different context. The Augustinian tradition, which was ultimately derived from Paul, in this respect had a similar influence
on both Luther and Erasmus. In the stark contrast made by Paul
between the 'spirit' and the 'letter' of the Law, contemporary
Jews were bound to suffer, if only theoretically. As the editor of
the relevant volume of the English edition of Luther's works has
observed, a similarly traditional view of Judaism may be found in
the lectures on the Bible which he composed in these years, that
is to say, on the Psalms, in 1513–15, and on Paul's Epistle to the
Romans, the text most susceptible to Augustinian interpretation, in 1515–16. In Shermann's words, 'the evidence
indicates that the Luther of these earlier years shared to the full in
the medieval prejudices against the Jews'.[18] It is clear that, unlike
Reuchlin, Luther, even at this early stage, did not defend the
Talmud against the charge that it contained blasphemy, and, in
addition, he also attacked the Kabbalah, as a pursuit for 'the
curious and the idle'. This was because his theological views on
the relative importance of faith and works (that is, deeds) in
achieving salvation had already developed sufficiently for him to
regard the Kabbalists' attempt to see divine power in Hebrew
letters as superstitious. At least in respect to the Jews, if nowhere
else, Luther followed the late-medieval 'nominalist' philosophy,
which, as ironically the Jewish Karaite movement had done since
the High Middle Ages, rejected all religion except that contained
in the basic literal meaning of the scriptural text. In Luther's
phraseology, Kabbalists, and in particular Christian cabbalists,
were attempting 'word-works', and were therefore engaged in an
illegitimate pursuit.[19]

These early expressions put into proper perspective the text of
1523, *Das Jhesus Christus eyn geborner Jude sey* ('That Jesus
Christ was born a Jew'), which has been regarded by some as
showing an earlier, positive view of Judaism, in contrast to the
later vituperation. Any careful reading of the text must surely
lead to the conclusion that, as in the period of the Reuchlin
affair, Luther did not, in 1523 envisage any legitimacy for
Judaism in the long term. The context in which the text was produced was in any case entirely within the Christian Church. At
the Diet of Nuremberg in 1522, Luther was accused of teaching
that 'Jesus was conceived of the seed of Joseph, and that Mary was

not a virgin, but had many sons after Christ.' This in itself makes it quite extraordinary that any scholar should have regarded Luther's defence as showing a positive view of Judaism as such. In the first place, the accusation puts into Luther's mouth words which express the conventional Jewish view of Christian teaching concerning the incarnation of Jesus and the virginity of Mary. The surviving records of the Spanish Inquisition abound in charges against converts from Judaism to Christianity who were supposed to have expressed such opinions. Naturally, Luther indignantly refuted the accusation, and he explicitly attacks what he quite correctly describes as a Jewish notion, concluding, after a rehearsal of the conventional material on the subject from the medieval disputations, that,

> If the Jews should take offence because we confess our Jesus to be a man, and yet true God, we will deal forcefully with that from Scripture in due time. But this is too harsh for a beginning. Let them first be suckled with milk, and begin by recognising this man Jesus as the true Messiah; after that they may drink wine, and learn also that he is true God.

The teaching which Luther aims to convey is thus quite clear. This is a conversionist text, aimed at persuading Jews that they will not suffer if they convert – though he should have hoped that German Jews knew nothing of what was then happening in Spain – so he states that,

> So long as we thus treat them like dogs, how can we expect to work any good among them? Again, when we forbid them to labour and do business and have any human fellowship with us, thereby forcing them into usury, how is that supposed to do them any good?

There is no denying the perceptiveness of the social observation in these lines, but it is equally undeniable that the whole policy proposed by Luther, apart from defending the writer from his fellow-Christians' accusations of heresy, was intended to show how Jews could be quickly and effectively converted to Christianity. Like his medieval predecessors, Luther believed that Adam

and the other Jewish patriarchs were really proto-Christians, 'and
so they were sustained through faith in Christ, just as we are'. It
should also be borne in mind that the whole of this text was
written out of Luther's desire for the reform of the Catholic
Church. Thus, when he considers the obstinate refusal of many
Jews to convert, he remarks, 'If I had been a Jew and had seen
such dolts and blockheads govern and teach the Christian faith, I
would sooner have become a hog than a Christian.'[20] In this respect, the Jews are being employed, as in the Middle Ages, as an
abstraction for use in a polemical debate, in this case about the
future of the Christian Church. There is, however, one other
interesting aspect to be considered in the 1523 text. This is the
single respect in which Luther's views do seem to have evolved
and changed over the previous ten years. He appears to have
moved from the relatively passive Augustinian view of the role of
the Jews in 'salvation history' and in human society which still
prevailed in contemporary papal policy, to the more active missionary attitude which had become prominent, particularly
among the Dominicans and Franciscans and with the anti-pope
Benedict XIII during the Great Schism, between the 1230s and
1500.

It is in this light that Luther's later, and increasingly violent,
anti-Jewish utterances should be understood. In the notorious
Von den Juden und ihren Lügen ('Of the Jews and their lies') of
1543, and in other passages from the letters and the table-talk, it
is precisely Luther's exasperation at the failure of the Jews to
respond by spontaneous mass conversion to the purification of
Christianity, which he and his supporters had brought about,
that produced the expressions of the crudest religious and social
anti-Jewish prejudice which are characteristic of the later writings
and speeches. In the table-talk recorded in 1539, Luther was still
able to admire King David for finding time to write the psalms,
while he was 'a husband, king, warlord, almost crushed by
political affairs and submerged in public business'.

However, the same source makes it clear that, by 1542–3,
Luther was fully equating the papacy and Catholics, from whom
he now saw himself as fully alienated, and the Jews. Both groups
'depart from the true Christian religion' because they teach
'"This I will do, and that will please God"', which for the

reformer was idolatry, whether practised by Catholics or Jews.[21] In thirty years, it was circumstances, rather than Luther's theology of Judaism, which had changed.

Calvin

The second most influential Christian reformer in the sixteenth and seventeenth centuries, John Calvin, had perforce, for most of his life, a somewhat theoretical view of Jews. At least until he was twenty-five, in his native Picardy, in Paris, Bourges and Orleans, he is unlikely to have met a Jew, while those of Geneva had been expelled many years earlier. Although he may well have had dealings with members of the community when in Strasbourg between 1539 and 1541, possibly even meeting the well-known German rabbi, Josel of Rosheim, his knowledge, inevitably, was mainly second-hand. There is also little sign that he knew much of Luther's writings on the subject, and he certainly did not know the German texts. None the less, in view of the considerable strength which was acquired by Calvinism in the later sixteenth century, it is important to piece together from his writings Calvin's attitude to Judaism as a religion.

The first point to notice is that the French reformer shared the conventional Christian view that, in the words of his main work, the *Institutes of the Christian Religion*, the Law and the prophets had been given to the Jews, so 'that they might turn their eyes directly to Christ in order to seek deliverance'.[22] Calvin remarked that 'all wicked men, as if conspiring together, have . . . shamelessly insulted the Jews'. Though the authenticity of the five books of Moses had never been doubted, yet he himself accused the Jews of falsifying passages in the prophets and later books. On the subject of that old warhorse of medieval Christian–Jewish disputations, the prophecy of Daniel, Calvin took Isaac Abravanel's commentary to task for failing to see the Christological significance of the text. Thus for him Barbanel (*sic*) was a 'dog' and an 'imposter', suffering from 'hallucinations'. Similarly, he was content to condemn the Jews as a people for their 'incredulity'. Although some Diaspora Jews had 'with them some seed of piety and the odour of a purer doctrine' (which of course meant Christianity), in a commentary on Jeremiah 19:9 ('The enemy will surround the city and try to kill its people. The siege will be so terrible that the people inside the city will eat one another and even their own children') he stated that such a savage treatment of the Jews by God was not surprising, since, 'if we compare the Jews with other nations, surely their impiety, ingratitude and rebelliousness exceeded the crimes of all other nations'. Also, Calvin accepted the concept of Jewish communal guilt for the crimes of individuals, a principle by then becoming obsolete in secular law and never admitted in the Catholic doctrine of penance. Thus he argued that the sale of Joseph into slavery 'could not be excused by Jews as having been but the crime of a few individuals. This infamy covers the entire people, for all the patriarchs, with the sole exception of Benjamin, dishonoured themselves equally by this perfidious act.' It was inevitable, therefore, that Calvin should have regarded the whole Jewish people, in the traditional medieval fashion, as collectively guilty of doing Jesus to death. In addition, like Luther, he had a strong tendency to group Catholics and Jews together, so that the ills of Catholicism, as he saw them, might be derived in part from the excessive influence of Judaism. On the social question of moneylending, the active role of his city as a financial centre did not deter Calvin from preaching in the strongest terms against Jewish usury. In sermons and commentaries, for example on Deuteronomy, he built up the picture of a Jewish people which had distorted the true meaning of the Lord's words through Moses, in order to exploit non-Jews, taking the 'occasion to ensnare all those who have little, for they interpret all the Scriptural promises to their advantage'.

Thus although Calvin did produce one systematic text on Judaism, the undated *Ad Quaestiones et Obiecta Judaei Cuiusdam Responsio* ('An answer to some Jew's questions and objections'), this, like his *Institutes*, sermons, and commentaries, does not go outside traditional Christian attitudes to Jews as religious and social beings, with a tendency towards imagining them as still on the pages of the Bible, rather than fellow-inhabitants of physical communities. There is one aspect of Calvin's thought, however, which may be regarded as somewhat innovative in relation to the Jews, though, as will be seen, its results were fairly limited. This is the question of Calvin's attitude to history. It was, of course, conventional for Christians to regard the Church as being the 'New Israel', taking over the promises, mission and chosen role which had belonged to the Jews by divine right before Jesus. Thus it is not remarkable that, while accepting that the Mosaic Law was given in order to prepare for the coming of Jesus, he should have seen much of it as worthwhile in the government and life of Geneva. The attachment to the Old Testament which is traditionally associated with Calvinism in contrast to the fastidious disdain of Erasmus, may properly be discerned in the works of the founder, but such an emphasis certainly did not necessarily benefit living, contemporary Jews. Of greater interest to the history of the sixteenth century was the view of his own followers which Calvin developed, in which they had a providential role similar to, and explicitly identified with, that of the Israelites of the Old Testament. Evidence for this may be found in sermons on Jeremiah and Lamentations, written in 1549, in the midst of the struggle and persecution of Calvinists.

> When then we see that we are like the Jews, we have a mirror in which to know our rebellion against God. . . . Thus, then, when we read this passage [Jer. 16: 1–7], let us learn not to condemn the Jews at all, but ourselves, and to know that we are not worth any more, and that if there was such brutality then that the word of God served for nothing, that today there is just as much [brutality] or more.[23]

At least this, and other comparable passages, avoid the customary contempt for Biblical Jews, which was so commonly extended to those still living, but it will be necessary to see, in later chapters, whether this rather more constructive attitude on the part of Calvin had any practical effect on Jewish life.

The general conclusion to be drawn from the writings and teachings of the leading reformers must be, however, that none of them significantly strayed from the medieval Christian traditions concerning Judaism and Jews. Whether the Counter-Reformation papacy and the Roman Church proved to be similarly unchanging and inflexible remains to be seen.

Notes

1 Helen Nader, *The Mendoza Family in the Spanish Renaissance, 1350–1550*, New Brunswick, Rutgers University Press, 1979.

2 J. N. Hillgarth, *The Spanish Kingdoms, 1250–1516*, ii, *1410–1516, Castilian Hegemony*, Oxford, Clarendon Press, 1978, p. 159.

3 Frances Yates, *Giordano Bruno and the Hermetic Tradition*, London, Routledge & Kegan Paul, 1964, p. 1.

4 John 4: 22.

5 S. W. Baron, *A Social and Religious History of the Jews*, New York/Philadelphia, Columbia University Press, Jewish Publication Society of America, 1976, xiii, pp. 163–4.

6 There is now a growing body of opinion among students of early modern 'popular' religion which is ready to blur the distinction between the respective beliefs and practices of educated and uneducated people. For a survey of recent work see the review article by John Edwards, 'The priest, the layman and the historian: religion in early modern Europe', *European History Quarterly*, xvii (1987), 87–93. Details of the almost infinite diversity of religious views, regardless of social class or level of formal education, which were found by the Inquisition in the Soria region of north-east Spain in the period 1450–1500, are provided and analysed in Edwards, 'Religious faith and doubt in late medieval Spain: Soria, 1486–1502', *Past and Present* (forthcoming).

7 D. P. Walker, *Spiritual and Demonic Magic from Ficino to Campanella*, London, Warburg Institute, 1958, repr. Neudeln/Liechtenstein, Kraus, 1969, pp. 82, 81. For an excellent general survey, see Brian P. Levack, *The Witch-hunt in Early Modern Europe*, London, Longman, 1987.

8 Gershom Scholem, *Origins of the Kabbalah*, ed R. J. Zwi Werblowsky, trans. Allan Arkush, Princeton, Princeton University Press and Jewish Publication Society, 1987, and *Major Trends in Jewish Mysticism*, New York, 1941, pp. 210, 212.

9 Yates, *Giordano Bruno*, p. 94.

10 Baron, op.cit., xiii, 175.

11 ibid., 175; Yates, *Giordano Bruno*, pp. 94–5; Baron, op.cit., xiii, 177–8.

12 Moshe Idel, 'The magical and neoplatonic interpretations of the Kabbalah in the Renaissance', in *Jewish Thought in the Sixteenth Century*, ed Bernard Dov Cooperman, Cambridge, Mass., Harvard University Press, 1983, pp. 189–91.

13 Heiko A. Oberman, 'Three sixteenth-century attitudes to Judaism: Reuchlin, Erasmus and Luther', in *Jewish Thought*, pp. 327–39.

14 ibid., pp. 340–2, 358–9n.

15 An important West German example of this activity is *Die Juden und Martin Luther. Martin Luther und die Juden. Geschichte, Wirkungsgeschichte, Herausforderung*, ed Heinz Kremers, Neukirchen-Vluyn, Neukirchener Verlag, 1985.

16 Alan Ecclestone, *The Night Sky of the Lord*, London, Darton, Longman & Todd, 1980, p. 18.

17 Dow Marmur, *Beyond Survival. Reflections on the Future of Judaism*, London, Darton, Longman & Todd, 1982, pp. 195–9.
18 *Luther's Works*, ed Franklin Shermann, vol. 47, Philadelphia, Fortress Press, 1971, p. 127.
19 Oberman, 'Three sixteenth-century attitudes', pp. 145–6.
20 *Luther's Works*, vol. 45, Philadelphia, Muhlenberg Press, 1962, pp. 198–229.
21 *Luther's Works*, vol. 54, Philadelphia, Fortress Press, 1967, pp. 340, 436–7.
22 *Institutes*, book 2. vi. 4, quoted in Baron, op.cit., xiii, 459n.
23 ibid., 279–96; Oberman, 'Three sixteenth-century attitudes', pp. 363–4n.

3
Jews in Italy and the Counter-Reformation

Although Protestant rulers were, in certain parts of Europe, having to devise policies for the independent control of religious life and expression within their territories, in the second half of the sixteenth century it was still the case that the old 'Roman' Church provided the main model for Christian–Jewish relations, and, through Catholic secular rulers, retained considerable influence over the practical conditions of Jewish life. It has already been seen that Rome and papal territories provided, in practice, a refuge for not inconsiderable numbers of Jewish refugees from the Iberian Peninsula. This indicated that the Augustinian attitude in medieval approaches to Jews retained considerable power in papal circles in the early sixteenth century, in contrast to the more militant 'conversionist' policy which had been advocated by many since at least the thirteenth century. None the less, things were, apparently, to change. Popes from Alexander VI to Paul III allowed refugees, not only from Spain and Portugal but also from Sicily and Provence, into their lands. Thus about half the Jewish population of Rome in the early sixteenth century had originated in Spain, Portugal, or Sicily. Paul III in the 1540s welcomed Jewish refugees from Naples into his port of Ancona, and allowed Spanish-speaking 'Levantine' Jews, that is, people who had emigrated to the eastern Mediterranean, to settle in Ancona, together with New Christians. However, Paul IV was to take a very different attitude. Scholars have viewed the Jewish policy of the popes in the ensuing years from varying perspectives, and it will be necessary to examine more closely both the theory and its practical results.

Jonathan Israel regards the period after 1550 as having brought about a major change in papal attitudes to the Jews. He refers to the 'anti-Semitic onslaught of the Counter-Reformation', describing the moves made by Cardinal Caraffa, later Paul IV, as involving a 'dramatic volte-face', which was 'inherent in the Counter-Reformation'. In view of the fact that expulsions of whole Jewish communities were a feature of European life, beginning with the English expulsion of 1290, Israel's claim that before 1450, 'no one spoke of the necessity of driving the Jews out' must clearly be disregarded. None the less, there is no doubt that, after 1553, pressure on the Jews did indeed increase, not only in Rome and the papal states but also in their other remaining places of settlement in northern and central Italy, and that the Church hierarchy played the main role in bringing this development about.

Before discussing the policy as such, it may be useful to look at the main events. The first sign of increasing Christian militancy in Italy was the burning, in Rome, of a Franciscan friar who had converted to Judaism. In August 1553 the papacy declared the Talmud to be sacrilegious and blasphemous, and therefore forbade its ownership and use. Major burnings of Hebrew books and manuscripts then took place in Rome, Bologna, Florence, Venice, and the Venetian colonies of Crete and Corfu. The next important measure was Paul IV's bull, *Cum Nimis Absurdum*, of 1555, which ordered the establishment of ghettos in all papal territories, on the model of that in Venice. In addition, the Pope reversed previous policy, which had allowed those forcibly baptized in Portugal in 1497 to revert to Judaism. Henceforth, such people were not to be safe in papal lands. A legate was sent to root out Portuguese New Christians in Ancona. In the Iberian tradition of avoiding the Inquisition, many fled to more friendly territory in the duchies of Urbino and Ferrara, but fifty-one were caught and sentenced, some of them to the galleys. Twenty-five were burned by the Inquisition in Ancona in April and June 1555.

The reaction of the Mediterranean Jewish communities to the Ancona deaths was strong. The Nasi, or Mendes, family, which had lived as Christians in Lisbon, Antwerp, and Venice but reverted to Judaism in Turkish territory, attempted to organize an economic boycott of the papal states, to the benefit of the duke of Urbino's port of Pesaro. But success in blocking Jewish trade between Italy and the Balkans was limited, since Pesaro was too far off the best route for cloth exports to the Near East from Florence, and, in any case, unbaptized Jews were bound to be harmed by the boycott too. In Italy itself, one of the traditional, occasional meetings of community leaders from the whole country was convened in Ferrara in 1554, to discuss the papal assault on the Talmud. It was decided that the Jews should offer to edit the text and commentaries, removing all the material which offended Christians; later, the fathers of the Council of Trent, then in session, were petitioned not to ban the Talmud *in toto*. Agreement on a compromise was eventually reached in the next papal reign, when the publication of a revised and expurgated edition was permitted in 1564, provided it did not bear the title 'Talmud'. The effect of papal pressure on secular states will be considered in due course, but the next significant move was made in 1569 by Pius V, in his bull *Hebraeorum Gens*. This expelled all Jews from the papal states, apart from Ancona, and thus ended dozens of communities, many of them ancient. Refugees left many places, such as Bologna, from which 800 were expelled, Orvieto, Viterbo, Forlì, Tivoli, Ravenna, and Rimini. It was intended that the measure should also apply to the French papal territories, but there were delays, and reduced communities survived in Avignon, Carpentras and a few neighbouring places.[1]

It is now necessary to look more closely at Israel's thesis that the policy of Paul IV, Pius V and other popes of the Counter-Reformation was 'not really a reversion to pre-Renaissance papal attitudes, but rather something basically new', 'a symbol of a new age'. There is no doubt that, as a result of the measures of 1553 and after, the papacy did succeed in bringing about a drastic deterioration in the conditions of Jewish existence in Rome and the papal states, in contrast to the days when the real-life counterparts of Delicado's *lozana andaluza* took refuge from the Spanish governments and Inquisition, more or less on the popes' doorstep. Kenneth Stow, the main student of papal Jewish policy in this period, describes *Cum Nimis*, for example, as a watershed in Jewish life in Italy. In order to assess this judgement, it is necessary both to seek the theoretical origins of the relevant papal pronouncements and to compare the practical conditions of Jewish life in Italy before and after the mid-sixteenth century.

The issue on which Stow concentrates in his survey of medieval papal pronouncements is the question of conversion, an issue which tended to separate the more and the less radical Christian views on the subject of the Jews. It is only with Martin V in 1425 that a greater sense of urgency begins to be discernible in papal pronouncements. Before that, the concern was merely to guarantee the survival of Jews, in restricted circumstances, in Christian society. Their conversion could safely be left to the end of days. There had been hints of a more active approach as early as 1278, when Nicholas III charged the Dominicans and Franciscans with the task of preaching to the Jews 'in order to remove the blindness of that people', but it was Martin V who explicitly stated, in his bull *Sedes Apostolica Pietatis*, that Christians received Jews into their territory 'under the hope of conversion'. For Stow, this text shows 'immediacy of expectation' of Jewish conversion, rather than 'the mechanically repeated prophecy of ultimate salvation' of earlier bulls. This policy of 'passive expectation', without any practical implementation on papal initiative, was to continue until the reign of Paul IV, though greater variations between the policies of succeeding pontiffs may be discerned during the fifteenth century. It is with Paul IV's bull *Cum Nimis Absurdum* that things appear to change, and the fact that Caraffa adopted that pontifical name may not be without significance, in view of the apostle's close but not always approving interest in his own Jewish people. In Stow's view, the conclusion of some early modern historians (and Israel seems to fall into the same category) that Paul's bull was a radical innovation is not justified by careful study of the text.[2] In reality, as Stow indicates, *Cum Nimis* closely resembles a canon of Lateran IV, *Etsi Judaeos*, which was repeated in a decretal of 1234, issued by Gregory IX. It was Gregory who also initiated the campaign against the Talmud so enthusiastically taken up both by secular rulers such as Louis IX of France and James I of Aragon, and by the Franciscans and Dominicans. This is hardly surprising, in view of the processes whereby the Roman Church habitually develops its teaching, or *magisterium*, and embodies it in ecclesiastical legislation. In this context, it is unwise to think in terms of sudden changes or developments of policy. Papal and conciliar legislation is never repealed but simply developed. In addition, the painstaking evolution of legal and bureaucratic procedures and habits in the Roman curia, at least since the reform movement of the eleventh century, had already, by the late Middle Ages, created a kind of ecclesiastical legal jargon or code in which words might have hidden meanings, or much deeper ones than appeared on the surface. Thus 'under the hope of conversion', in Martin V's bull, might well contain, in coded form, an acknowledgement of the great movement of conversion to Christianity which followed the anti-Jewish violence in Spain in 1391, and even imply a recognition of the deep preoccupation of the defeated anti-pope, Benedict XIII, with the eschatological conversion of the Jews.

In reality, the measures taken by Paul IV did not arise out of nothing. In 1543, Paul III set up a 'house of converts', or *domus catechumenorum*, in Rome, having written a few days previously of his hope that the Jewish community would 'return to the way of truth'. Paul III's policy was supported by all succeeding popes in the period, and Stow explicitly points to the thirteenth-century origin of the concept of the house of converts, which was clearly linked with measures to separate Jews from Christians. The foundation bull issued by Paul III in 1542, *Cupientes Judaeos*, indeed repeated the provisions of earlier bulls of Nicholas IV in 1278 and John XXII in 1320. The house of converts was intended to answer a preoccupation, also already shown in the thirteenth century, with the danger that Jews who converted to Christianity would lose financially, through the confiscation of their property by secular rulers. The other danger seen by the Church was that converts would relapse, through continuing contact with the Jewish community. This perceived danger had been one of the main factors, as has been seen, in the decision to expel unbaptized Jews from Spain in 1492. It also preoccupied the Counter-Reformation popes. Thus Jews were required to finance the house of converts, at the rate of ten ducats from each synagogue in 1554, for example, though in view of the declining wealth of the communities under his rule Gregory XIII agreed to lower the charges due. The house was intended not only as an incentive to Jews to convert – hence the granting to its members of full civil rights – but also to keep them away permanently from their old communities. That this danger was far from abstract may be seen not only from the Spanish evidence but also from an incident which took place in Cremona, then under Milanese rule, in 1469. In this case, eleven Jews from the town and elsewhere were arraigned before the duke of Milan by his *podestà* in Cremona for creating disturbances outside the convent of San Benedetto and the bishop's palace in the town on Good Friday and Holy Saturday. They were protesting against the baptism of Caracosa, the wife of Solomon of Viadana. The case is complex, involving the woman's being kidnapped by her prospective Christian husband, an outlaw in Pavia. After much conflict between ecclesiastical and secular authorities, the compromise reached was that the baptism stood, but that the Jews were absolved of their offences, which had apparently included the singing of obscene songs about the nuns.[3] The incident illustrates not only the deep hostility of Jews to the conversionist activities of the Church, but also a certain self-confidence on their part, which possibly arose from their knowledge of the conflicts which existed between the clergy and local government officials. In the sixteenth-century papal states, of course, such a conflict of jurisdiction and interest did not exist. The catechumens were to be well educated, and to be encouraged to marry non-Jewish Christians, from whom they might learn to forget their old, Jewish ways. This particular aspect of papal policy will be of great interest in the context of the whole question of crypto-Judaism, such as that which caused the violent repression of Portuguese New Christians in Ancona. At this stage, however, it is mainly necessary to note the dominance of the conversionary aim over all papal policy. It is also interesting to observe the role of the founder of the Society of Jesus, Ignatius Loyola, in encouraging the sixteenth-century revival of the house of converts. He appears to have appreciated the missionary potential of such an institution, and to have suggested the 1542 scheme to its public proponent, the rector of San Giovanni de Mercato.[4] The only apparent exceptions to the conversionary policy were Sixtus V's bull *Hebraeorum Gens* of 26 February 1569, which reversed Pius V's expulsion order against Jews in the papal states, and *Christiana Pietas*, which once again allowed the publication of the Talmud, without that title. Indeed it permitted the re-edition of 'all Hebrew books', though this latter measure was never implemented and in fact, Sixtus V did not go against what had been decreed by Paul IV, as amended by Pius IV.

Naturally, various attempts have been made to account for the strengthening of papal measures against Jews, even if they cannot, in truth, be regarded as innovations. One explanation is to be found in the context of what was happening to Christianity in the mid-sixteenth century. Visible Christian unity was under severe threat, and Europe appeared to be increasingly full of enemies of the Catholic faith. In this situation, Judaism the oldest enemy of all, might well appear even more threatening than before, especially in view of the flirtation of various Renaissance intellectuals, including churchmen, with Jewish Kabbalah. In earlier times the Church authorities had tended to link the Jews with Christian heretical movements, such as Catharism, and it was therefore tempting to suppose that an alliance might develop between the rebels in the sixteenth-century Church and the old Israel. This may have been believed, even though the evidence now clearly shows that the Reformers did not significantly differ from Catholics in their attitude to Jews and Judaism.

However, there is another aspect of papal policy at the beginning of the Counter-Reformation which deserves attention, and which provides a further link with medieval thought and policy. This is consciousness of an imminent end to the world, which generally led, in the later Middle Ages, to militant efforts particularly by friars to convert the Jews – for example by means of the thirteenth- and early fourteenth-century missionary schools of Ramón Penyafort and Ramón Lull, and the conversionary campaigns of Vincent Ferrer in the years after 1391 in Spain. In the case of Paul IV, the sixteenth-century pope most associated with the revival of restrictions on Jews and attempts to convert them, there is clear evidence of preoccupation with the last days, as indeed there had been in the earlier case of the anti-pope Benedict XIII who had sponsored Ferrer's preaching. Stow has assembled evidence which indicates that Caraffa had a strong eschatological mentality, even before he became pope. According to his correspondence with his sister, he had already, in the 1520s, abandoned all hope for the future of the world, and was concentrating on his personal salvation which he believed to lie in the monastic vocation. His despair at what he and many contemporaries saw as the ever-increasing violence and cruelty of both individual men and states may be compared with that of one of these contemporaries, Erasmus, though the latter's humanistic values dictated a very different response. Neither view, however, offered much hope of peace to Jews. The future Paul IV also seems to have had a strong personal belief in the Devil, such as was common among all social classes and at all levels of education. He apparently regarded heretics as agents of the Antichrist, who according to Scripture, was to appear at the end of days. In May 1547, when reformed Christianity appeared to be spreading out of control in Europe, Caraffa urged his sister to study the apocalyptic prophecy of the seventy weeks in Daniel, chapter nine.

> Read it if you wish to see the despair of our times. One cannot read it without tears; of it one can say it describes so clearly our state. But if the great mercy of God does not aid us, then we ourselves must be expeditious. Indeed the clemency of that great Lord who said, 'From the time of John the Baptist, the kingdom of heaven submits to force, and the violent may seize it', is the sole reason I do not despair completely, because such great strength has been conceded to me that I am capable of making that violence on heaven.

The links between private letters and public policy may be somewhat tenuous, but it is difficult not to see the influence on Caraffa's actions as pope, of the frame of mind which he described to his sister in a letter on 24 August 1549.

> I am now aged, but I never permit myself an hour of repose, in addition to the infinite sorrows which I perceive at every minute, to see in this unhappy time the ruin of the world and the subversion of the faith, and to hear from every side the bad news, in the way that the messengers of Job kept arriving

without one waiting for the next. Worse, with all this huge
blaze, there is no one who, for the zeal of God, has the desire
to toss on it sulphur and wood. We have surely arrived at that
calamitous moment about which my most holy father [Peter]
in his second epistle prophesied, saying, 'In the end of days,
false, deceiving men will appear, acting according to their own
wilfulness; and for you they will be false teachers who will
introduce the sects of perdition; and many will go in the way of
their viciousness, and through them the way of truth will be
blasphemed; and in avarice, through false works, they will
make commerce of you.'[5]

It seems fairly clear that Paul IV did believe himself to have a personal mission to help the Lord to hasten the coming of the last
days, of which the conversion of the Jews was to be a sign.

The practical effects of the policy initiated by the popes in the
1540s and after inevitably departed somewhat from these exalted
theological notions. However, in legal terms, too, there was a significant change in the conditions of Jewish life in the papal territories in the second half of the sixteenth century. First of all, in
1550, Julius III decided that civil and criminal cases which
involved Jews should go to the papal vicar for decision, while
Sixtus V extended the power to hear such cases to all bishops,
lords, and governors in these lands. The thought behind this
change, which apparently ended the traditional internal legal
autonomy of Jewish communities under Christian rule, was
openly expressed by Clement VIII in *Caeca et Obdurata* on 25
February 1593, in which he stated that the Jews, who were described traditionally, in the first words of the text, as 'blind and
obdurate', had abused the 'privileges' which had been offered to
them in the hope of their conversion. Clement decided that this
'obduracy' had gone on long enough, and expelled all Jews,
except those who remained in Rome, Ancona, and Avignon
under close and conversionary supervision. The rest were to leave
within three months, or else lose all their goods and be condemned to the galleys. The monitoring of Jews in Rome, mentioned in Clement VIII's bull, became increasingly close after the
establishment of a ghetto. Typical of the legal conditions under

which Jews lived in late sixteenth-century Rome was the renewal of existing legislation by the papal vicar-general, Cardinal Rusticucci, in August 1592. Jews were not to allow Christians into their synagogues, they were not to enter the houses of Christians, except those of judges, advocates, and notaries; they were not to receive Christians into their own homes after midnight, or to eat or drink with Christians, except while on journeys; they were not to sell meat or unleavened bread to Christians or slaughter animals for them, in case this were done in accordance with Jewish ritual; they were not to teach Christians the Hebrew language, or the liberal arts (this measure being, in itself, an indication of the assimilation of Jews to Christian culture which in fact existed in Renaissance Italy), or the techniques of sorcery (which perhaps refers to Kabbalah); they should not have Christian servants, or bath or shave with Christians, or wash anywhere except in the river beside the ghetto; they were not to employ Christian mid-wives or wetnurses, tutors, executors, or guardians, and they were not to attend Christians as physicians; they were not to lend money to Christians or play them at games; they were to wear visible yellow badges on their hats and they were to be subject to a curfew between the first hour of the night and daybreak. The 'Lozana' would hardly have flourished in such an environment, and, although it is very doubtful that all these laws were actively or efficiently enforced, it is none the less clear that, in the late six-teenth and seventeenth centuries, they caused many Jews to suffer financial penalties, or sentences in the galleys, or else to convert, in order to avoid such punishment.[6]

The secular Italian states had never allowed themselves to be governed by ecclesiastical policy in their treatment of their Jewish inhabitants. In the sixteenth century, areas under Spanish rule or influence gradually followed the Iberian example, and expelled their Jewish communities, but many rulers, even when under pressure from Spain, attempted to continue the indigenous tradition of Jewish–Christian relations. In Raffaello Morghen's words,

Jewish civilisation in the Middle Ages [in Italy] did not live separately and alien from contemporary Christian civilisation, but within a common tradition of spirituality and thought . . .

and it identifies with the history of a people and religion that was given a very definite juridical and moral status and treated, if not on a completely equal footing with other religious confessions, at least with a great deal of understanding and tolerance.[7]

To this, Toaff adds that social and economic interests could in effect make relations between the two communities even closer, if not necessarily more friendly. Modern studies of important areas of Jewish settlement in central and northern Italy in the late Middle Ages, such as Assisi, Mantua, and the large duchy of Milan, indicate the fragility of such relations between the Jewish minority and the Christian majority. Both economic and religious difficulties were constantly liable to affect Jews in these territories, and compound the problem of their always ambiguous legal status. A typical example of the legal complexities is the position of Jews in the duchy of Milan. Apart from religious tradition and social prejudice, Jewish communities were also affected by the convoluted legal history of Italy as a whole. A juridical vacuum, after the fall of the western Empire, had gradually been filled by self-appointed legal authorities attempting to take on the mantle of the Romans, and in particular by the papacy and what came to be called the 'Holy Roman Empire'. However, by the late fifteenth century, both had long since retreated, totally in the case of the Empire, and had been replaced by effectively independent, largely seigneurial, states. The vital legal question, in relation to Jews was, what authority would replace the Empire, and with what result for their status and conditions of life? Along with some other Italian *signorie*, the dukes simply took over the Imperial prerogatives and legal formulae in their own territories. These had little or no relation with the ecclesiastical tradition and canon law procedure which shaped the papal policy of the sixteenth century. In the Milanese lands in Lombardy, therefore, the Jews were regarded as the *servi camerae*, the slaves or serfs of the ruler's chamber, just as they had been by the Emperors, and still were by monarchs elsewhere. They thus depended on the ruler for their rights and privileges, indeed for permission even to live in his territory. These rights were normally enshrined in legal agreements, or *condotte*, which, by the fifteenth century, had become largely standardized. In late medieval and early modern Milan, they normally guaranteed Jews the right to inhabit a certain town and its surrounding *contado*, or territory, freedom to trade and make banking loans, to worship and govern their own communities internally. Jews subject to a *condotta* were guaranteed legal protection by the duke and, if it ever became necessary for them to leave a certain area, as increasingly happened towards and after the year 1500, then in this case too they were to be protected by the government.

The Jewish population of the duchy of Milan went through many vicissitudes in the period between 1350 and 1580. In the late fourteenth century, the territory became a refuge for emigrants from other parts of western Europe, such as France and Germany, as well as less hospitable areas of southern and central Italy. Later, there were immigrants from Spain too. The attitude of Milanese rulers also fluctuated somewhat in this period. The Visconti and Sforza dukes generally favoured the grant of *condotte* to a large number of local communities, and the ducal archives indicate the establishment of seventeen new Jewish settlements between 1400 and 1450. Expansion of the number of settlements continued until the 1480s, when decline began, along with local expulsions. Under French rule after 1494, and in the period of the last Sforza after 1535, Jews returned to many areas, despite Spanish political influence. Paradoxically, Shlomo Simonsohn estimates that there were more Jews in the duchy in the period of Spanish dominance than there had been in the fifteenth century, with the Jewish population probably reaching its peak in the 1560s and 1570s. The clear impression given by the charters and other documents assembled by Simonsohn is that successive dukes were generally closely involved, on a personal and day-to-day basis, with the affairs of their Jewish subjects, and that they endeavoured, within the prevailing legal and political constraints, to protect Jews, and, in particular, favoured doctors, bankers and even engineers, from the hostility of the Christian majority. Such activity was pragmatic in character, and a similar picture emerges from Michele Luzzati's studies of Jewish life in Tuscany, where independent republics, or city-states survived into the Renaissance period. In the approach, for example, of the

republic of Lucca to the issue of Jewish settlement, which he describes as 'the notorious and age-old diffidence of the republic of
Lucca not only in confrontations with Jews, but with foreigners in
general', Luzzati discerns a careful balancing of public and
private, internal and foreign policy interests, through which Jews
managed to survive, and not without personal success. In other
cases, external powers intervened to influence the policy of states
towards Jews.[8] In Pisa, for instance, a brief moment of freedom
from Medici control, as a result of the French invasion of 1494,
allowed the Florentine rulers' tolerance of Jews, particularly in
the banking sector, to be temporarily ended, but the return of
the Florentines in 1509, and of the Medici themselves in 1512,
restored the old situation. Other special local arrangements
applied in towns within the papal states, such as Assisi, where,
since the fourteenth century, Jews had been subject to the jurisdiction of the Christian authorities, the *podestà*, the *capitano del
popolo*, and the criminal judges, in the same way as other inhabitants. *Condotte* made with bankers in 1401 and 1456
showed similar equality of status between Jewish and Christian
financiers, and the *podestà* often referred cases to joint commis-
sions of Jews and Christians for decision. Entirely Jewish cases
might be referred to the rabbinical court in Perugia, thus, in a
sense, giving the Jews the best of both worlds. Jews in Assisi were
simply not distinguished legally in the manner prescribed by the
Church and most medieval secular states. Their testimony, under
special but not demanding or insulting oaths as sometimes
happened elsewhere, was admitted in court on the same basis as
that of Christians and their signatures appeared on notarial documents, which often, inevitably, also involved non-Christians.
The local bankers' contracts show that, in effect, there were no
limits on the property which might be held by Jews, including
arable land. Pragmatism seems to have broken taboos and overcome religious and secular scruples.[9] Thus the general social state
of the Jews in northern and central Italy, before the Counter-
Reformation, is well illustrated in the approach of Luzzati, who
proposes that,

> an analysis that includes the various social and cultural levels,
> independently of the fact that they are Jewish or Christian

milieus, would seem to open the way to a more flexible enquiry, and one corresponding better to the actual facts of the history of Italian Jews in the last centuries of the Middle Ages.[10]

The same is certainly true of the sixteenth and seventeenth centuries. While taking a fairly hostile attitude to the behaviour of his co-religionaries in this period, in contrast to the neutrality, or even approval, of Luzzati, Shulvass none the less has to show the extent to which practice differed from theory in Jewish–Christian relations. This phenomenon affected both communities. Thus:

> The rapprochement between Jews and Gentiles and the partial integration of Jews in Christian society also deprived the Jewish communal institutions of much of their significance. . . . There was no real religious transgression in patronising non-Jewish courts in a land and period where the social barriers between Jew and Christian were few and Jews trusted non-Jewish judges.

Worst of all, in Shulvass's view, the Italian Renaissance period saw a threat, from assimilation, to Jewish family life. There are some significant statistics in Shulvass's account, for example that 40 per cent of the indictments against Florentine Jews in the fifteenth and sixteenth centuries were not for economic offences but for sexual relations between Jewish men and Christian women. Jewish women, too, sought both irregular and regular liaisons with Christian men. Shulvass disapproves of all marriages not arranged by parents within the Jewish community, but he does confirm the existence of Jewish prostitution among native Italians as well as the Spanish Lozana and her friends. For him, the picture was one of regrettable disintegration, in the face of pressure from the Gentile world.

> On the one hand the Jewish family steadfastly clung to deeply rooted traditional patterns. On the other hand, throughout the entire period we encounter individuals who attempted to destroy accepted family patterns to satisfy their romantic

desires. . . . They . . . often brought upon themselves untold suffering. They became victims of the Renaissance desire to tear down the barriers that separated man from man.[11]

It is very unlikely that this perspective is correct (see chapter 5 pp. 137–42), since Christian and Jewish rules of religious and social conduct were all notoriously likely to be broken in many and varied times and places. In addition, it almost certainly exaggerates the impact of the Renaissance, presumably seen here as a cultural phenomenon, on Italian social life. However, the main problem with this material is the obstinate refusal of the evidence to provide adequate demographic statistics. In the case of Jews, all that is left is the occasional local and temporary figure, normally in terms of households rather than individuals. The policies of the popes of the Counter-Reformation thus brought about a deterioration in the conditions of life for native and immigrant Jews alike. If these policies are to be set in their social, as well as their religious context, it is necessary to consider two important features of Christian–Jewish relations in the late fifteenth century which framed the conditions for the popes' actions and also provided them with a theoretical context. These phenomena, which by 1500 had become almost universal in all areas of Jewish settlement in Italy, under whatever kind of political constitution, were the conversionist and anti-Judaic preaching campaigns of the friars, and the linked attack on the economic role of the Jews in Italian society through the movement for the establishment of banks, known as *Monti di Pietà*, to make small loans to the poor. The strictly Christian activities of preaching and missionary work among the Jews, as well as efforts directed at the raising of the levels of Christian understanding and practice of the Gentile laity, were special tasks of the Dominican and Franciscan orders of friars. Their influence on the fate, not only of Christian heretics but also of Jews in various parts of western Europe is well known. However, in Italy in the fifteenth century, a new aspect of Christian opposition to Judaism developed, in an even more directly social form than missionary work. In fact, the thinking behind the *Monte di Pietà* movement was at least as much social as religious in motivation. The Church, first in Italy and later elsewhere, had long since come to terms with the activity of moneylending, or usury, although it was forbidden by the Bible, but financial services to the smooth flow of international trade had a very different effect on society from the petty loans and pawnbroking which constituted the contact between most individuals and the financial sector. The fact that Jews, despite the overall diversity of their activities in the Italian economy, were none the less associated, both in religious stereotype and in practical experience, with moneylending, especially to the population at large, made them an obvious target for the friars and their supporters, the latter including people of all social classes and occasionally the governing authorities. Thus one motive for the conversion or expulsion of the Jew was his role as, in Attilio Milano's words, 'a supporter of a regime of economic oppression that distressed the people'.[12] To this, in Toaff's opinion, might be added in certain areas, such as Assisi, a tendency to disparage Jews for their close collaboration with seigneurial regimes elsewhere, of which Milan was a conspicuous example. The friars in the fifteenth and early sixteenth centuries took advantage, as secular rulers had done in earlier centuries, of a genuine grievance in order to advance their own religious aims, which went much further than the popes had so far done in the direction of eliminating Judaism by means of conversion. Thus the friars exploited, or even provoked public protest against usury,

> ably directing all the discontent of the times of grave and frequent economic crisis in their direction, or else enlarging on [the Jews'] small frauds. More than fighting an image, they were the ones to create it, agitating the spectre of plague and famine or threatening excommunication.[13]

There is much truth in this observation. As Brian Pullan has clearly demonstrated, mid-fifteenth-century interest rates offered by Jewish financiers were likely in fact to be lower than those of their Christian colleagues. Thus, in Brescia in the 1440s, the Christians seem to have been charging as much as 60 to 80 per cent, while Jews, conscious no doubt of the prejudice against them, as well as being perhaps more efficient, were offering rates of 20 or 25 per cent.[14] Evidence from other northern Italian towns, as well as from the relatively obscure Brescia, indicates the willingness of many local and ducal authorities to allow Jews to fill gaps in the credit arrangements for the majority of the inhabitants of their territories. This pragmatic and practical state of affairs was not, however, to last. The first major figure to launch a significant generalized attack on the Jewish money-lender's role in society was Bernardino of Sienna, whose fame spread from his own Tuscan region after 1417. He toured the country, denouncing usury in general and Jewish usury in particular, and his Franciscan order took up the campaign. The normal pattern of relations between the friars and the papacy, since the thirteenth century, had been one in which the friars took the initiative and the papacy followed reluctantly, if at all. Such a process has already been demonstrated in the theological and practical question of the conversion of the Jews. In the case of Jewish moneylending, a similar pattern was followed. The reformed wing of the Franciscan order, known as the Observants, had failed to persuade Martin V to support its measures to eliminate the Jewish usurer, partly because of effective Jewish lobbying, a tactic to which the papacy in this period was usually susceptible. However, the efforts of Bernardino and of Giovanni di Capistrano, the first and second vicars-general of the Observants, had better success with Eugenius IV, who was also subject to anti-Jewish pressure from John II of Castile and who issued the bull *Dudum ad Nostram* in 1442. This bull forbade usury by Jewish moneylenders and ordered restitution of interest previously taken, as well as laying down other measures directed at the separation of Jews and Christians in their social lives. Although the measure appeared at first to be directed at Spain, it is clear from the confirmation by Calixtus III in 1456 that it was also meant for Italy. Whatever the rights and wrongs of accusations made against Jewish moneylenders, it was necessary, if they were to be banned, to replace them with some other method of providing credit to ordinary people. It was to solve this problem that the Franciscans devised the notion of the *Monte di Pietà*, a suitably pious title for a bank which was to be under Christian control, intended to put the Jews out of business, and which, in the words of the eighteenth-century Jesuit, Francis-Xavier Zech, consisted of 'a certain fund of money (or of other consumable goods) collected together for the assistance of the poor, to be lent to them on the security of pledges'.[15] The scheme therefore involved loans at little or no interest at all, and its appeal to Church, local authorities and clients was obvious. Bernardino of Sienna's preaching against Jewish moneylenders had lacked impact because he did not provide an alternative to their services. He had achieved considerable papal support, however, and was canonized in 1450 only six years after his death. It is perhaps no accident, therefore, that the first *Monte* which functioned in the manner later to become standard was established in Perugia, in the papal states, in 1462. The religious context could not have been clearer. In Lent of that year, the Observant Franciscan Michele Carcano preached a series of sermons, in which he asserted that, 'the city of Perugia is excommunicate on account of the agreements it has made with the Jews to encourage the poisonous crime of usury and will remain so until these concessions are rescinded and annulled'.[16]

After this, Franciscan efforts spread *Monti di Pietà* through central Italy between the Apennines and the Adriatic, in Umbria and in the Roman Marches. Despite at first becoming a casualty of the traditional rivalry between the Franciscans and the Dominicans, a project for a *Monte* in Florence eventually succeeded, during Savonarola's maverick reign, in the 1490s. By then such institutions had been established for nearly twenty years in other Tuscan cities such as Sienna, Pistoia, and Prato. Popes were by this time confirming the statutes of individual banks, but still provided a loophole for opposition from the Dominicans and others by failing to issue a bull confirming the general *Monte* principle. By the 1480s, *Monti* had been established in the mainland towns under Venetian rule, in many cases at the urging of yet another strong-minded Franciscan, Bernardino Tomitano of Feltre. The question of Jewish life in Venice itself, however, needs special consideration in view of its great importance in the fate of European Jewry as a whole, and of the rich and well-researched archives which exist in the city.

It is, of course, Venice which has the dubious honour of having given the word *ghetto* to the world, thus adding to what Brian Pullan calls 'the vocabulary of persecution'. Since the war of the League of Cambrai in 1509, Jews from Venice's mainland territories had been taking refuge in the city. Their immigration also brought for the first time an effective manifestation of the Franciscan religious and economic campaign against the Jews. The friars warned of the 'corruption of the state' which would result from allowing the Jewish refugees to stay, but the Venetian authorities did not wish to lose the financial services which the Jews were still providing, seeing that there was no *Monte* in the city itself. The answer to the problem of 'contagion' which might pass to the Christian population was thus to follow the example of various other European cities since the twelfth century at least, and confine Jewish residents to a specific quarter of the city. Here it was the so-called 'Ghetto nuovo' – 'new foundry' in Venetian dialect – which was ideally suited for the task, in that it had solid walls and a single entrance and could be guarded at night by the Council of Ten's police. Thus, although the term 'ghetto' itself was merely topographical, the social meaning behind it was clear from the start. The establishment of the ghetto came mid-way through the operation of a *condotta*, and when this expired in 1519, the whole issue of Jewish settlement in Venice was opened up again. The two main conflicting arguments, one economic, in favour of the retention of the Jews, and the other religious, advocating their expulsion, were recorded in contemporary sources. According to one side in the debate, the Jews should remain because they 'are necessary for the sake of the poor, since there is no *Monte di Pietà* here as there is in the other cities', while the others argued that God's favour would only rest on the 'most serene republic' if they were expelled, since,

> it would be good to expel them from the whole world, and God would prosper this Republic as he did the king of Portugal, who, on expelling them, discovered the new route to India, and God made him the king of gold. Even so did the king of Spain permit such great wealth to depart from his country, for the sake of exiling these devourers of Christians and enemies of Christ.[17]

In the event the ghetto survived and was indeed added to, in a limited and belated response to growth in population, with the establishment of the Ghetto Vecchio in 1541 and the Ghetto

Nuovissimo in the 1630s. The foundation of the original ghetto inevitably caused much upheaval. It removed Venice's Jews from the parishes close to the central markets and the Rialto, in which they had originally settled, placed them in relative isolation from the economic heart of the city, and disrupted the lives of the Christians who had to make way for them, though Gentile land-lords were conveniently compensated by the payment of rents a third higher than those demanded of the former Christian tenants. There were, of course, other 'foreign' quarters in the city holding Turks, Greeks, Germans, and other nationalities, but the Jewish community was different in that it was confined by compulsion, not bound together voluntarily for mutual protec-tion or economic convenience. All the Venetian ghettos were extremely overcrowded. The best estimate indicates that there were twice to four times as many inhabitants per hectare in the Jewish quarters as in the rest of the city, and this inevitably led to a poor social environment. 'Levantine' Jews, that is, those who came to Venice from the Ottoman empire, having in many cases originated in Spain and Portugal from families which became Christian, complained in 1576 that the Ghetto Vecchio had 'become by day and night a den of thieves and harlots, troubled by rows, clashes of weapons, and threats'.[18] The same might be said of the other ghettos, but the complexity of the social struc-ture of Venetian Jewry, apart from providing, as it were, a microcosm of European Judaism in the period, did allow many individuals and families a certain mental, if not much physical, space in which to develop their lives. By about 1600, there were three main 'nations' of Jews in Venice, the 'Germans', who were by this time effectively Italian, the Ponentines, who came from Spain, Portugal, or the Low Countries, and the Levantines, already mentioned, who came from the eastern Mediterranean. There is however another aspect of the Venetian Jewish community which raises considerable questions about the influence of the Spanish and Portuguese expulsions on Jewish life in sixteenth- and seventeenth-century Europe. This is the presence in Venice of individuals who had, at one time, been baptized as Christians. The Ponentines commonly came into this category and might be variously known as New Christians, converts (*conversos* in the Iberian languages), or even as Jews,

because many reverted to the old religion, often during an intermediate stay in Turkish-ruled territory between periods in their
western countries of origin and their eventual arrival in Venice.

The origins of the word *marrano* have still not been satisfac-
torily established, although it is clear that, in its use by Christians, it was intended as an insult to converted Jews, or,
importantly, their descendants, who failed to become entirely
orthodox Christians. According to one common interpretation,
there are connotations of 'swine' in the word, although in Jewish
circles, partly as a result of the work of Cecil Roth and Israel
Révah, it has now become a badge of honour for those who
supposedly maintained the Jewish faith even after outward conversion to Christianity. Such people were, of course, the stock in
trade of the Spanish (and from the mid-sixteenth century the
Portuguese) Inquisition, and a relatively small number of such
cases appear also in the records of the Venetian tribunal, in the
period after 1548. However, the complexity of the Venetian
situation at this time exposes the dangers of generalization about
the religious experience of individual people. It is simply too
easy, and hence misleading, to offer standardized descriptions of
the religious attitudes and practice of those converted from
Judaism to Catholicism, and in particular about 'the reactions of
Jews to the experience of forced conversion [as in Spain and
Portugal] and to that of living in strongly conformist countries
where open adherence to Judaism was forbidden'.[19] The
subtleties of the evidence to be found in the Venetian Inquisition's trials of 'judaizers', which have been edited by Ioly
Zorattini and analysed by Pullan, make it impermissible to
indulge a belief in abstracts such as 'the Jews', 'the Christians',
or 'the *marranos*'. In a chapter on *marranos* as both Catholics and
Jews, often, as in the earlier Spanish case, at the same time,
Pullan found that,

> the spectrum which began with the convinced Jew has ended,
> seemingly, with the convinced Christian. Parents' religious
> decisions were sometimes – who knows how often, or how
> rarely? – challenged by their children: sometimes in a spirit of
> experiment, sometimes in a spirit of disgust. Sometimes we
> have seen individuals striving, with different degrees of

determination, for a religious identity of their own in the face of heavy family pressure, from parents, uncles or other kinsmen.[20]

This must surely be the proper approach to Jews, or converted Jews, who arrived in Venice, often after extraordinary personal odysseys, to find their religious convictions tested by the very freedom which the city offered, in contrast with most of the rest of Europe. Individual reactions to this state of affairs were inevitably as diverse as the characters of the persons involved. Thus, in Ioly Zorattini's words, it is necessary to avoid tackling the subject of 'marranism' 'like something unitary, and reducible to a single matrix'. Rather, the material should be seen as 'evidencing, beyond the language of the trials, which is always reductionist and schematic, a religious reality which is quite rich and complex'.[21]

Certainly, the notion of a distinctive *marrano* religion, based on the Old Testament rather than rabbinical interpretation of the Bible, and existing behind a façade of Catholic conformity, does seem to be the fabrication of scholars, though their number may include a few unrepresentative figures in the early modern period itself. On the other hand, while it is impossible to convey in a short space the riches of human experience offered by the Inquisition trials, especially of Spain, Portugal, and Venice, it may be useful to quote just a single personal story to illustrate the role of Venice in the life of so many Jews or ex-Jews in sixteenth- and seventeenth-century Europe. This is the tale of the 'wandering Jew of Illescas', as the nineteenth-century Spanish scholar Father Fidel Fita named him.

Some time in Lent 1514 (1 March–15 April), a man went to make his confession in the Dominican church of St Peter Martyr in Toledo, after having heard a sermon. He was referred to a Hieronymite friar in the royal foundation of St John 'de los Reyes', but no confessor was available when he presented himself there on the following Easter Sunday, and 'he had a row with the porter, because he did not give him anyone to confess to'. Outside the church he told his tale to another man, and was directed to a priest in yet another church. He, however, refused to act, because it was 'a matter for the inquisition'. Eventually, after further attempts by the potential penitent to obtain an ordinary confession, the Holy Office did indeed take on the case, and the resulting statement, though without the record of a trial, survives. The story is complex and absorbing, though by no means untypical of the experience of those Spanish Jews and converts who found themselves at the mercy of religious and political developments. On 15 May 1514, the inquisitor of Toledo ordered the interrogation of 'a blind man', called Luis de la Isla, who described himself as 'a New Christian of Jewish origin', aged about thirty. His former name was probably Abraham, as he was later known thus, outside Spain. He was born in Buitrago, brought up in Illescas, and fled the Toledo area rather than convert to Christianity in 1492. Between then and his eventual return, over twenty years later, Luis alias Abraham travelled almost everywhere in the Mediterranean area. He fled first to Algiers, and then lived, still as a Jew, in Venice, before moving to Genoa and converting to Christianity. Having changed his religion, he was free to return to Spain and did so, learning and taking up the trade of a silk-weaver. However, by 1506 he was in Italy again, still travelling from place to place, and it was through his work that he met Jewish colleagues in Ferrara and began to hanker after his old religion once more. From then on, he seems to have been looking for a chance to 'come out', and eventually did so in Turkey's Adriatic possessions, finding, thereafter, increasing numbers of individuals who had also come from Spain and rediscovered their roots in places in the eastern Mediterranean where Judaism could be practised freely. He thus lived as a Jew in Venice, Salonika, Adrianopolis, Constantinople, and Alexandria, where local Jews tried to make him give up his Christianity altogether, and stop fluctuating between one religion and another. This confrontation with the demands of the old orthodoxy seems however to have had a negative effect, as Abraham became Luis once again and lived as a Christian thereafter. He made his confession to two friars in Egypt, one of them from the church of the Holy Sepulchre in Jerusalem, and it was after this that he returned to Spain, via Naples, and in effect turned himself in to the Inquisition. The story is complex, individual, and somewhat anarchic, but it gives vivid testimony to the religious confusion in which so many in these centuries lived on the borders of Christianity and Judaism, and to the diverse personal solutions which might be found in places such as Venice and the Ottoman empire where genuine choices of religious affiliation might be made.[22]

At this stage, however, it is necessary to return to the realm of high politics, and consider the response of the Venetian government to the presence of its Jewish community, as well as the social policy of other Italian rulers. Levantine Jews had been allowed to stay temporarily in Venice since 1541, when, apparently following the example of the duke of Ferrara, the authorities decided to act in order to regain trade with the Turkish empire via the Balkans, which was increasingly in the hands of Jews of Spanish and Portuguese origin. The economic motive of the new policy, which also gave the Inquisition an entrée to Jewish life in the city, with results which have already been noted, seems fairly obvious. In Israel's words, 'Indeed, so it seemed, no Italian ruler with an eye on the Levant traffic could afford to hold back from the scramble to attract Levantine Jews.'[23]

The Medici grand dukes of Tuscany gave ample privileges in 1551 to Sephardi merchants involved in the trade between Pisa and the Balkans, via Ancona and Pesaro. Papal policy, from Paul IV onwards, did however have a temporary effect on the activities of Tuscany and other states, including Venice and Urbino. It reduced their willingness to accommodate New Christians, in the knowledge that they might well be involved, more or less secretly, with Judaism. The climax of Christian triumphalism in the later sixteenth century was the victory over the Turks at Lepanto in 1571. In the euphoria of the moment, the Venetians actually proposed the expulsion, not only of the Levantines, but also of all Turks and their subjects. Some were probably frightened enough to depart, although the 1571 expulsion was allowed to lapse. In the event, opportunities for Jews in northern Italy tended to improve in this period, despite the unpleasantness in the papal states. For one thing, the duke of Savoy, having followed Genoa's example and expelled his Jews in 1560–1, changed his mind in 1565, and not only invited the exiles back, but also took in refugees from papal territory in Avignon and Italy. Finally, in 1572 he issued a charter, described by Israel as 'sensational', which invited not only Levantines but also other

New Christians to come and help develop his port of Nice as a trading outlet for the Levant and as a centre for textile manufacture. It contained the vital guarantee that the Inquisition would not be allowed to interfere. After a great deal of pressure from Spain and the papacy, the duke gave in and withdrew the privilege in 1574, though he none the less took in many of the 900 Jews expelled from the Milanese in 1597. The Jewish communities in Savoy, including Turin, Asti, and Nice, all seem to have expanded in the last third of the sixteenth century. Venice allowed Levantines back in from 1573 onwards, and now also officially condoned the arrival of New Christians, including refugees from Ferrara, after the papacy had secured the arrest there by ducal officials of some Portuguese believed to be 'judaizing'. Venice had always, as Pullan clearly shows, been extremely reluctant to admit outside ecclesiastical authority within its territory, and especially in the city itself. Based on these traditions, the late-sixteenth-century governments defied the papal policy more openly than other states such as Savoy and Ferrara felt able to do. The printing of Jewish books in Spanish was allowed to resume in the 1580s, after a gap of about thirty years, and in 1589 the Senate officially recognized the three 'nations', German, Levantine and Ponentine, the last being a fairly transparent disguise for the Spanish and Portuguese *conversos*.

The evidence does indeed seem to support Israel's contention that economic motives increasingly defeated religious pressures in the northern Italian states, in the period up to and beyond the year 1600. The 1589 Venetian privilege, which seems to have resulted in part from the advocacy of a Dalmatian of Spanish origin, Daniel Rodríguez, led to the development of the overland routes between the Adriatic and Turkey, about a fifth or a third of the trade being in the hands of Sephardic Jews. By 1600 the Jewish population of the Venetian ghettos had risen to about 2,500, compared with only 900 in 1552. It appears that *conversos* from Portugal, emigrating after the Spanish increased the activity of the Portuguese Inquisition in 1580, now preferred to go to Venice and Tuscany, where the grand dukes increasingly defied the popes and developed a new port at Livorno. An anomaly occurred, whereby Jews in Venice and Florence still had to live in ghettos, like those in most of Italy, while those who went to the developing ports, such as Pisa and Livorno, were not subject to such restrictions. In addition to Savoy, Venice, and Tuscany, Jewish populations also grew in Padua, Verona, other parts of the Veneto and Friuli and, in particular, Mantua. Simonsohn's researches show that the Jewish population of the latter city grew from about 200 in 1500 to 960 in 1587, and to no fewer than 2,325 by 1610, making it one of the four or five largest communities in western Europe.[24] Religious considerations may have triumphed in the papal states, but in the north the economy had the upper hand. The period after 1600 indeed saw the continuance of these policies, to such an effect that those known as 'Portuguese Jews' came to dominate the trade of Venice, Pisa, and Livorno, at the expense and to the annoyance of Christian merchants and commentators in both Venice and Florence. The wider European debate about the role of the Iberian 'Jews' will be considered in due course.

Notes

1 Jonathan Israel, *European Jewry in the Age of Mercantilism, 1550–1750*, Oxford, Clarendon Press, 1985, pp. 16–23.

2 Kenneth R. Stow, *Catholic Thought and Papal Jewish Policy, 1555–1593*, New York, Jewish Theological Seminary of America, 1977, pp. xxiii–xxiv. For the view that Paul IV did innovate in his policy towards the Jews, see, for example, Cecil Roth, *The History of the Jews in Italy*, Philadelphia, Jewish Publication Society of America, 1941, pp. 296–8.

3 Shlomo Simonsohn, ed., *The Jews in the Duchy of Milan*, vol. 1, *1382–1477*, Jerusalem, Israel Academy of Sciences and Humanities, 1982, pp. xxiii, 468–77, 484–5, 492–3, 496.

4 Stow, *Catholic Thought*, pp. 11–12, 52–4.

5 ibid., pp. 262–7.

6 A. Bertolotti, 'Les juifs à Rome aux XVIe, XVIIe et XVIIIe siècles', *Revue des Etudes Juives*, ii (1881), 278–89.

7 Raffaello Morghen, *Medioevo Cristiano*, Bari, Laterza, 1974, pp. 146–7, in Ariel Toaff, *The Jews in Medieval Assisi, 1305–1487. A Social and Economic History of a Small Jewish Community in Italy*, Florence, Olschki, 1979, p. 9n.

8 Michele Luzzati, 'Lucca e gli Ebrei fra Quattro e Cinquecento', in *La Casa dell'Ebreo. Saggi sugli Ebrei a Pisa e in Toscana nel Medioevo e nel Rinascimento*, Pisa, Nistri-Lischi, 1985, p. 170.

9 Toaff, *Jews*, pp. 73–8.

10 Translation in Toaff, *Jews*, p. 9n.

11 M. A. Shulvass, *The Jews in the World of the Renaissance*, Leiden, Brill, 1973, pp. 49, 55, 159.

12 Attilio Milano, 'Considerazioni sulla lotta dei Monti di Pietà contra il prestito ebraico', in *Scritti in Memoria di Sally Mayer*, Jerusalem, 1956, p. 205, quoted in Toaff, *Jews*, p. 57.
13 Toaff, *Jews*, p. 59.
14 Brian Pullan, *Rich and Poor in Renaissance Venice. The Social Institutions of a Catholic State, to 1620*, Oxford, Blackwell, 1971, p. 445.
15 Quoted in Pullan, *Rich and Poor*, p. 451.
16 ibid., p. 453.
17 ibid., p. 489.
18 Brian Pullan, *The Jews of Europe and the Inquisition of Venice, 1550–1670*, Oxford, Blackwell, 1983, p. 157.
19 ibid., p. 201.
20 ibid., p. 228.
21 Pier Cesare Ioly Zorattini, *Processi del S. Uffizio di Venezia contro Ebrei e Giudaizzanti (1548–1560)*, Florence, Olschki, 1980, p. 16.
22 Fidel Fita, 'El judío errante de Illescas (1484–1514)', *Boletín de la Real Academia de la Historia*, vi (1885), pp. 130–40.
23 Israel, *European Jewry*, p. 45.
24 Shlomo Simonsohn, *History of the Jews in the Duchy of Mantua*, Jerusalem, Ktav, 1977, pp. 191–3.

4

Jews under Catholicism and Protestantism: the Netherlands, the Empire, and Poland

The Netherlands

When Jews began to return in numbers to western Europe in the latter part of the sixteenth century, the Netherlands quickly became their most important single area of settlement. The phrase 'Dutch Jerusalem' came to be used about the seventeenth-century community in Amsterdam which, apart from achieving a significant role in the regional economy, also accompanied the Dutch colonizers worldwide and provided the first members of the restored Jewish community in England. The rise of Dutch Jewry, towards 1600, was not however the result merely of re-immigration from the east. Jewish influence, in a fairly hidden form, had not been entirely absent from the Low Countries in the period between the late medieval expulsions and the achievement of independence by the United Provinces. This was due to the activities of exiles from the Iberian peninsula, and it is with them that the story of early modern Dutch Jewry must start.

In historical terms, it was natural that individuals and families who fled from Ferdinand and Isabella's expulsion edict of 1492, or from the programme of forced baptism in Portugal in 1497, should have chosen to go in the direction of the Netherlands. In the major trade patterns of Europe after the Black Death in the mid-fourteenth century, there had been a pronounced development of the importance of the maritime route from the Mediterranean to England, the Low Countries, and north Germany, via the Spanish, Portuguese, and French coasts.

Clearly, the Mediterranean was still, in the fifteenth century, more sophisticated economically than the Atlantic coast or the North Sea, and so Mediterranean mercantile expertise, in particular Genoese, tended to operate a trade which used Iberian carriers, mainly Andalusian, Portuguese and Basque. Thus the products of the south of Spain and Portugal, such as corn, olive oil, tunny-fish, wine, fruit, silk, cochineal, sugar, wax, and leather, as well as the vital precious metals of which Spain was the most important distribution centre in the period, would be transported on a route to the English Channel and the North Sea. Stops to pick up goods would be made in, for example, Almería, Málaga, Cádiz, and San Lúcar de Barrameda as ports for Seville, Lisbon, and further halts for trading purposes in, for example, Bayonne, La Rochelle and Nantes, before arrival at destinations such as Southampton, London, and Antwerp.[1] In addition, there was a land 'axis' between the interior of Spain and the Netherlands, dominated increasingly by the merchants of Burgos, which involved mainly the export of merino wool to the cloth-manufacturing towns of the Netherlands and the import of the finished cloth, to the great detriment of the native textile industry. The dynastic connection between the two territories, made by the marriage of the Emperor Maximilian's son Philip, to Joanna, daughter of Ferdinand and Isabella, merely ratified politically a strong existing economic trend, which Spanish and Portuguese discoveries and colonization merely served to underline ever more firmly.

Some Sephardic refugees settled in French ports. Spanish and Portuguese New Christians (for in theory there should have been no professing Jews in France by this time) settled, early in the sixteenth century, in the suburb of Saint-Esprit, across the river from Bayonne, though they were not given official permission to do so until 1550. It is clear, though, that some of the settlers and their descendants were actually practising Jews, there and in smaller places nearby such as Bidache and Peyrehorade. In other cases, however, the Spanish and Portuguese *conversos* did not begin to settle noticeably in France until the seventeenth century, when they appeared for a while in Nantes and Rouen, though the Nantes immigration seems to have consisted of some of those expelled from Bayonne in 1636. Small numbers of

Sephardic refugees also settled in Bordeaux, beginning what was later to become a prominent Jewish and crypto-Jewish community. The small numbers there and in Bayonne were granted letters patent by Henry II in 1550, giving them royal protection in return for their contribution to trade and industry. By the 1570s, however, the religious wars in France seem to have created sufficient confusion for Jewish religious practices to have become somewhat more overt, a fact which was officially disregarded by Henry III in his new letters patent of 1574. Immigration of New Christians, which had begun to grow in the 1570s, increased further when the Portuguese Inquisition redoubled its efforts against 'judaizers' after the monarchy was united with Spain. By the 1590s, Jews, or New Christians, according to popular and official designations respectively, had reappeared also in Paris, and in 1595 Henry IV guaranteed the right to practise Judaism in one of the newer French acquisitions, Metz.[2]

In the Netherlands, on the other hand, there were officially no Jews at all by 1549, except in Antwerp where Iberian trading contacts were by this time strongest, following the decline of Bruges. The actual religious practice of the Spanish and Portuguese in Antwerp is still a controversial matter, probably because the complexities of the religious life of the Iberian peninsula were reflected in the refugees. As in Spain and elsewhere, the Inquisition became involved with New Christians in its quest for heresy, but the Netherlands tribunal, which was set up by Charles V and the pope in 1522, seems to have arisen from the threat of 'Lutheranism', rather than the importation of judaizing *conversos* from the Iberian peninsula. The background to the New Christian immigration to Antwerp was the transfer of the Portuguese merchants' 'factory' from Bruges in 1499. By this arrangement, the Portuguese could govern themselves, under privileges which the Emperor and the city government combined to provide. The numbers suspected of Jewish belief and practice up to 1549 were small, and, although the Imperial government from time to time incited the general population by means of poster campaigns to attack 'judaizers', economic interests generally kept safe any '*marranos*' there may have been in the city. According to Révah, nearly all the New Christians who came to Antwerp after 1526 were fleeing from the Inquisition. Some of them were indeed tried as judaizers by the Netherlands tribunal. However, over-ruling the protests of the local authorities, in August 1549 Charles V ordered the expulsion of all New Christians who had come to the city in the previous six years, confirming the edict in 1550. The immigrants were to leave within a month, and were also banned from Brabant, Flanders, and Zealand.[3] According to Goris, whose view is repeated with greater caution by Geoffrey Parker, a significant number of Antwerp's New Christians converted to Calvinism when that option became available around 1560.[4] Révah strongly disagrees, however, seeing the Antwerp 'Portuguese' community as the usual Iberian *converso* mixture of 'judaizers', to varying extents, and genuine Christians. The words of Provost Morillon to Philip II's minister, Cardinal Granvelle, in September 1566, support this assessment.

> It is said that the Portuguese are strongly infected [with Calvinism], and for this cause are as agreeable to the people of Antwerp as the Spaniards are odious. But, certainly, I believe that they are Jews, and that they care little about our religion, but that they are very happy to present themselves as such so as to nourish all the more dissension in our holy faith.[5]

The test of the religious allegiance of the Antwerp 'Portuguese' was not so much their conduct under Spanish rule as their response to the arrival of William of Orange in 1577. Crypto-Calvinists might have been expected to appear in the open in the new climate of religious freedom, but the *conversos* did not. Perhaps Révah exaggerates the Jewish practice of these individuals, being one of those scholars who believe in 'marranism', but there is no particular reason to suppose that Calvinism would have appealed to the Iberian New Christians, and Morillon was merely expressing the age-old belief that Jews wished to undermine the Christian faith.

It is, none the less, worthwhile to consider the impact of the religious upheavals which took place during the 'Dutch revolt' on the possibility of leading a Jewish life in the Netherlands. In principle, the fragmentation of political authority and the separation of large numbers of Netherlanders from the Catholic Church might have led to greater religious freedom for Jews and an end to the need for any 'judaizing' Iberian *conversos* to conceal their true beliefs. To understand what actually happened, it is necessary to look at the background to the Netherlands Reformation and its relationship to the battle against Spanish authority. Although the traditional episcopal inquisitions and the state-run tribunal set up by Charles V had been attempting to oppose Lutheran influence since the 1520s, Calvinism, which was to become by far the most influential form of Protestantism in the Netherlands, only began quite late to achieve an impact. Its doctrine was first condemned, as such, in Charles V's 'blood edict' against heresy in 1550. Even then, there were no Calvinist churches in the Netherlands until 1555–6, and still only twenty in 1561, compared with the hundreds in France. It appears that support for the sudden upsurge in Calvinist activity, and in particular the smashing of religious images in Catholic churches which took place in many towns in 1566, was not doctrinaire in nature. The level of pastoral care in the Low Countries had never been high, as Toussaert's study of religious life in late medieval Flanders clearly shows. Episcopal coverage was thin, and the arrival of Spanish authority under Charles V merely served to alienate much of the population even further from the Church. None the less, Luther and Calvin's theological views do not seem to have had a wide appeal in the sixteenth century. Most Netherlanders' interest seems to have been more in reforming abuses in the existing Church and achieving the independence from Spanish influence of indigenous political institutions. Thus, although the preaching meetings and iconoclasm of 1566 displayed a spectacular enthusiasm, Calvinist theology did not yet have deep roots in the country. Phyllis Mack Crew has shown that popular indifference, rather than mass support, gave an opportunity for a small highly-motivated group of Calvinist leaders to send gangs of youths about their destructive task.[6] Visible support for Calvinism quickly declined when the chance of a reconciliation with Spain appeared. None the less, the political and religious upheavals of the 1560s and 1570s did provide the potential for greater religious toleration if only by default.

It is indeed the thesis of Jonathan Israel, one of the leading scholars of Dutch Jewry in the seventeenth century, that the impact of the religious wars of the sixteenth century on the theory and practice of religious freedom was very great. In his view, despite the fact that so few modern historians are religious believers, 'there is still . . . an almost universal disinclination to focus attention on the progressive weakening of Christian belief in early modern times'.[7] If this epoch-making development is properly taken into account, then the improvement in Jewish conditions at the end of the sixteenth century, in the Netherlands and elsewhere, becomes more comprehensible. According to this theory, the break-up of medieval Christendom, as a religious and a social entity, also involved the removal of the medieval policies for the treatment of Jews. When Christians had to learn to tolerate diversity within their own ranks, they discovered in the process that they could bear believing and practising Jews among them too. There are, of course, difficulties in taking the concept of 'toleration' as the thread which runs through early modern religious and social policy. Henry Kamen gave, years ago, a clear definition of the word: 'In its broadest sense, toleration can be understood to mean the concession of liberty to those who dissent in religion.'[8] He indicates his view of the process whereby religious, racial, and social intolerance may be defeated when he stresses the need to avoid treating the subject as though it were no more than an aspect of the history of ideas, when, in reality, there is no continuous and inexorable progress from intolerance to tolerance, and when no religious thinker or leader could ever function outside his own social and political environment. The case of the Netherlands during the Dutch revolt also seems to indicate a need to distinguish between toleration as an active principle and policy, and toleration as the *de facto* and unintended consequence of a power vacuum.

It seems fairly obvious that the situation in the Netherlands falls into the latter category. To begin with, there is no sign that practical Calvinism was of any greater benefit to the Jews than the theories of the founder. Crew points out that a Calvinist minister in the mid-sixteenth-century Netherlands, struggling to evangelize a fairly inert and conservative population, and at the same time to avoid arrest, might well regard himself as a descendant of the Old Testament prophets, 'with the licence to chastise kings and to predict the destruction of tyrants and the triumph of the chosen people'. However, the evidence shows that such leaders continued to regard living Jews in the traditional Catholic way, making the customary equation between the negative portrayal of the Jews in the New Testament, and the Catholic clergy of their own day. For Guy de Brès, in a petition to Philip II, they were,

> successors of the Scribes and Pharisees, who, under this title of church, of the great holiness of the temple of God . . . have given themselves licence to corrupt the true service of God. And for this cause, the prophets banded against them . . . [and] destroyed their synagogues and assemblies at Sodom, Gomorrah and Babylon.[9]

If the Calvinists usurped the theological role of certain Old Testament Jews in this way, it is hard to see how contemporary Jewish merchants and artisans could benefit. In fact, though, the conflict with Spain and between Catholics and Calvinism seem, in most cases, to have created only confusion. First of all, in Parker's words,

> After decades of neglect from the old church and a mounting tide of anti-clerical criticism, many people appear to have become spiritually disorientated and ready to rally to any authoritative figure who could reassure them about the after-life and salvation.[10]

He goes so far as to suggest that the 1570s saw in the Netherlands an 'almost complete breakdown of Christian order'.[11]

What practical effect, then, did this state of affairs have on Jewish life in the region? In the first place, it appeared to many at the time that the opposing forces, both secular and ecclesiastical, had fought themselves to a standstill. In the process, the religious landscape in the country had become considerably more varied than most of the countryside. There were now, alongside those who adhered in however lukewarm a way to Catholicism, some remaining Lutherans, a gradually growing but still somewhat scattered Calvinist laity – which a more motivated and organized clergy was attempting to shape into permanent, institutional churches – and other more radical believers, known indiscriminately and disapprovingly to both Catholic and mainstream

Reformed Christians as 'Anabaptists'. It might be thought that Iberian refugees, experienced in concealing their activities from skilled and determined investigators (such as the royal account-ant (*contador*) Alonso del Canto who pursued suspected Spanish Protestants to the Netherlands in the early 1560s), could have achieved effective freedom in such conditions.[12] In the event, the circumstances of Jews and New Christians with Jewish tendencies did indeed improve after 1570. It has already been noted that the main southern community, in Antwerp, remained at least notionally Catholic during the period of William of Orange's control from 1577 to 1584, but some indication of the true nature of religious belief and practice among the 'Portuguese' in the city may be found in the declaration made in 1585, after the Spanish had reoccupied the city, by Baltasar da Costa, a *converso*. The statement was, of course, made under special circumstances, in that Da Costa had returned to Portugal and was making his con-fession to the Inquisition there. However, he did say that he had been guilty of Jewish practices along with all the other New Christian families in Antwerp, except for 'the house of Ximenes, the house of Rodrigues [de Evora], related to the Ximenes, and Luis Enriques', a native of Oporto.[13] In Révah's view, conditions remained thus in the Catholic Netherlands throughout the seventeenth century. One consequence of the successful war of independence of part of the Netherlands was that the rest re-jected the Inquisition, which had been one important reason for the rebellion in the first place. This of course meant that the detection of 'judaizers' was left in the hands of the bishops and the local authorities, and even the reformed Tridentine episcopal hierarchy, which had been introduced amidst such controversy in the 1560s, could not seriously pursue '*marranos*' in the areas which remained under its control.

The situation in the newly-independent provinces seemed even more hopeful, despite the fact that, at the moment when the Spanish shackles were thrown off, Jewish life in that region was vir-tually extinct. It is difficult to disentangle religious from economic motives, in the new authorities' attitudes to Jewish settlement and activity. Business acumen was clearly much needed. The need to maintain the edifice of Catholic policy towards Jews was hardly paramount in areas which had just defeated the greatest Catholic

Jews under Catholicism and Protestantism   101

power in Europe after a lengthy struggle. In addition, Calvinism owed its very existence to liberty of conscience, as well as to political and military struggle. In practice, there was no prospect of establishing a new 'state church' in the Dutch provinces. For one thing, many of their inhabitants, not least among the population of Amsterdam, which was to defeat Antwerp and become the new economic capital of all the Low Countries, showed a marked reluctance to abandon the Catholic faith. A certain liberty of religious conscience thus seemed desirable on various counts, including that of public order. In their declaration of 20 July 1572, the States-General declared a halt to all violence between religious groups. Although, in the following year, public Catholic worship was forbidden, priests were not to be molested, any more than the adherents of other churches including Lutherans and even the dreaded Anabaptists. The magistrates were to permit people to believe what they liked, provided they did not cause a 'scandal' or endanger public order. Thus the breakdown in practice of Christian order, to which Parker referred, was effectively given the blessing of the new Dutch government. In the southern Netherlands, on the other hand, the Dutch attack of 1576 temporarily drove the 400 or so 'Portuguese' from Antwerp. Thus began the Jewish revival in the independent north as many refugees, who did not go to Cologne in the relatively safe Holy Roman Empire, migrated to such places as Middelburg and Rotterdam. Most, however, returned to Antwerp as soon as it was safe to do so. In the following year, Antwerp city council, conscious of the economic value of an openly Jewish population, went so far as to ask the Frankfurt community to send some of its members to the Low Countries. There was no immediate result, but Jews did, in the 1570s and 1580s, begin to settle in Groningen. The most significant long-term development, however, was the settlement of the 'Portuguese' in Amsterdam. Although exact numbers are not known, there were probably 200–300 New Christians in the city by 1600, the community thus rapidly approaching the size of that in Antwerp. The attitude of the Amsterdam bourgeois to the settlement of these immigrants, all shrewdly suspected of being Jews behind a mask of Catholicism scarcely necessary in the religious situation of the United Provinces, was considerably less hostile (governed as it was by the overall economic interest of the city) than the attitude of the Venetian oligarchs to *converso* immigration. The Amsterdam notarial records of the period between 1595 and 1620 clearly show that the city's trade increasingly and lucratively concentrated on Portugal and the Portuguese colonies, and it is fairly obvious that the economic and social connections of the 'Portuguese' *conversos* were being used to enhance the economic prosperity of the 'Dutch Jerusalem'. All was not straightforward, however, for actual or potential 'judaizers' who attempted to establish themselves in Amsterdam. In accordance with contemporary Spanish custom, the city's artisan and trading guilds would not admit them as members, clearly regarding them as Jews rather than Christians, despite their baptism. Thus although they played an important part in securing imports of sugar, Brazil-wood, and Indian diamonds, via Oporto and Lisbon, from areas in which the Dutch East India Company had no active interest, the 'Portuguese' in Amsterdam were restricted, in Israel's words, to 'a flourishing, if somewhat narrow, craft sector'.[14] In addition, in contrast to Venice, the Amsterdam city fathers did not allow public Jewish worship, there being no ghetto, and in 1604–5 the Venetian Sephardic immigrants to Amsterdam asked to be transferred to Haarlem and allowed to build a synagogue there. In the event, Rotterdam made this concession first, in 1610, but the deal fell through and two years later the seven Jewish families which had moved to the city in anticipation of freedom of public worship, returned defeated to Amsterdam. At this stage, the Spanish still found it possible and worthwhile to send agents to foment anti-Jewish feeling among the city's Calvinists, and it appears that they helped to secure the abandonment in 1612 of a project to build a synagogue, after it had been started. The edifice was not to be completed until 1639.

It was in the early seventeenth century that the local authorities of the independent Netherlands, and their States-General, began to debate the issue of public Jewish worship. Significantly, Hugo Grotius's paper to the States-General continued the traditional Christian rejection of Judaism as a valid religion, but it none the less advocated the grant of permission for Jewish settlement on economic grounds. Christians, according to Grotius, were to be kept away from the potential attractions of Jewish worship. Jews were to be forbidden public office, their shops were to remain closed on Sundays and holy days, and there were to be no conversions of Christians to Judaism or sexual relations between adherents of the two religions. The only aspects of Grotius's proposals which were not entirely in accordance with papal teaching, at least from Innocent III to the Counter-Reformation, were his failure to forbid segregation of Jews' and Christians' living-quarters, and his willingness to condone the employment of Jews as shopkeepers and artisans on the same basis as the majority population. Grotius's paper had no immediate result, but during the seventeenth century the possibilities for a full Jewish life in the Netherlands gradually increased. During the Thirty Years War, between 1618 and 1648, some Ashkenazi Jews moved westwards, but there were too few to form a separate Netherlands congregation until 1635, and there was no organized community life until after 1660. The effect of the war on Dutch Sephardic interests was at first drastic, in that they were no longer permitted to trade with their traditional contacts in Portugal, but by the year 1700 they had effectively re-established themselves in trade with America. Between 1630 and 1654, Dutch colonization in Brazil gave them an important opportunity but, by the end of the century, in Israel's words, 'what had once been a trading network based overwhelmingly on Lisbon and Oporto finally ended up, after a series of dramatic oscillations and upheavals, as a system based essentially on Curaçao, Surinam and St Eustatius'.[15]

In the second half of the seventeenth century, there were, for example, about 4,000 openly practising Jews in Amsterdam. This population had doubled by 1700, mainly as a result of German immigration, so that about 4 per cent of the city's population in that year was Jewish, thus constituting the largest concentration of Jewish inhabitants west of the Balkans. Sephardic success in the colonial trade enabled Ashkenazim to make inroads also into crafts and trades, such as jewellery, precious metals, tobacco, and spices. The Sephardim came to dominate the diamond, sugar, chocolate, and tobacco trades, and by 1700 the Amsterdam community was governed by three boards, one each for the 'Portuguese' and 'High Germans', established by

1639, and the third for immigrants from Poland, who arrived, as a result of upheavals in their own country, later in the century. Still, at the end of the seventeenth century, the old Iberian mixture of genuine Christians and 'judaizers' of varying kinds existed among the descendants of the original *conversos*. By this time, significant Jewish settlements also existed, for example, in Friesland and in Amersfoort, which had become one of the main Dutch Jewish communities. Thus by 1700 in the Netherlands, the economic argument does seem to have finally overcome religious considerations, though it would be rash to assume that all the accompanying social, or even theological, prejudices were thereby removed.

The Empire

After the many local expulsions of the period between 1470 and 1520, it did not appear that prospects for Jewish life in the Holy Roman Empire could be other than poor. However, German politics were never simple. The main figures who helped to ensure the continuity of Jewish settlement in the Empire, despite all pressures to the contrary, were, on the Jewish side, the leading rabbi in Germany, Josel of Rosheim, and, on the Christian side, the Emperor himself. Although Charles V was the main source of attempts to remove heresy, including 'judaizing', from his Netherlands territories, he and the remaining Catholic rulers in Germany, especially the prince-bishops, became the protectors of Jews against attack, above all from Protestants. Indeed, the record of the newly-Lutheran rulers in their treatment of their Jewish populations was not good, merely continuing the medieval tradition of hostility and expulsion, which had only been supported by Luther's own attitude to Judaism and Jews. Thus Jews were ordered to leave Saxony in 1537, and certain Thuringian towns such as Mühlhausen in the 1540s; there were riots in Brunswick in 1543, and further expulsions took place in 1553 from the duchies of Brunswick, Hanover, and Lüneburg. Trouble developed in the margravate of Brandenburg in the 1560s, and the Berlin synagogue was attacked in 1572. In 1573, a second expulsion of Jews from the whole of Brandenburg took place, and the pattern of hostility, leading to expulsion, was repeated in 1582 in Silesia, with the exception of three communities. To this it may be added that the practical attitude of Calvinists to Jews was very similar. The main Calvinist state in Germany, the Palatinate, had 155 Jewish families in 1550, but the Jewish population was expelled in 1575 by the Elector Frederick III.[16]

On the other hand it seemed, by various actions, that the Emperor wished to halt the exodus of Jews from Germany, so that, paradoxically, they were safer in states with Catholic rulers. The fact that Jews were technically under Imperial protection had not prevented violence and expulsions under Maximilian I, but Charles V, without apparently deviating from the traditional attitude towards the Jews which formed part of the medieval heritage which he devoted his life to upholding, seems to have concluded that he and his supporters needed the help of Jews in order to defeat the burgeoning Protestantism.[17]

The Imperial diets of Augsburg in 1530 and Speyer in 1544 were used to confirm the protected status of Jews in the Empire, but the most important measure taken by Charles V's government to protect the Jews was included in the 1555 Augsburg religious settlement. This explicitly excluded the Church states, ruled by prince–bishops, from the otherwise general rule that the prince should decide the religion of each state. The object of this move was to prevent any prince–bishop from becoming Protestant and turning the state into a conventional Lutheran principality, with consequences which might include the expulsion of the Jews, as was increasingly happening in existing Lutheran areas. As Israel points out, the result was that Jews duly remained in the countryside of the archbishopric of Cologne, though not in the city itself, where the medieval expulsion was allowed to stand. They also stayed in the bishoprics of Münster, Minden, Halberstadt, Paderborn, Würzburg, Bamberg, and Speyer, and in the abbatial principality of Fulda. The response of Jews to Charles V's protection was immediate and positive. Josel of Rosheim, for example, soon recognized Luther as an enemy, but called the emperor 'an angel of the Lord'. The Jews supported Charles in the war of the Schmalkaldic League in 1546–7, and prayers were even offered at that time for the Emperor in Frankfurt, although the Imperial free city was on the Protestant side. Material help was also given, in the form of financial subsidies and loans, and wagons and provisions for the Imperial army.[18] In return, Charles endeavoured to protect Jews from attack, for example by his Spanish troops who did not apparently understand why their king, in, for example, Castile or Aragon, should behave so differently in his role as Emperor. As there was no other part of his empire in which he adopted such a positive attitude towards the Jews, it can only be concluded that pragmatism, rather than inner conversion, was mainly responsible for the anomaly.

After the abdication of Charles in 1556, and the division of the Habsburg lands, the accession of Ferdinand I had left German Jews in more or less the same situation, but this could not be said of Jews in the kingdom of Bohemia, which was an electoral territory within the Empire. Here, as further west, the growth of Protestantism brought about a deterioration in the Jewish condition which, this time, the Emperor appears to have supported, adopting a policy similar to that of Spain. There had already been a major outbreak of anti-Jewish violence for example in Raudnitz and Saaz in 1541, and in Bohemia, in contrast to the policy then current in Germany, Jews were subsequently expelled from all the Crown's towns except for Prague, the capital. In 1557, the new emperor agreed to complete the expulsion in Bohemia itself, by ordering the Prague community to leave. Neighbouring Moravia was, however, unaffected, apparently because the nobles had sufficient power and influence in that area to overcome the anti-Jewish policy of the towns – a situation which might be compared with that in Poland and Lithuania. However, the collapse of Jewish life in Bohemia was not quite completed when Ferdinand's son succeeded him, as Maximilian II, in 1564. A few Jews had managed to survive in Prague. What would have been hard to predict at the time was that Bohemia between 1564 and 1612 was to become one of the most remarkable centres of religious and social life for Jews and Christians, under the emperors Maximilian II and Rudolph II. Before considering the implications of the Bohemian experience for the religious and intellectual history of Europe, it is, however, advisable to look first at the practical results of the two emperors' policies towards Jews, both in the kingdom of Bohemia itself and in the Germanic lands which were subject to their influence.

The growth of the Prague community, from its low point in the early 1560s, was slow. In 1570, there were still only 413 Jewish households, perhaps about 2,000 people, in the whole kingdom of Bohemia. It soon became clear, however, that the new Emperor had a very much more positive attitude towards the Jews and Judaism. An important source of evidence for the change is the work of the Prague Jewish chronicler, David Gans, who lived through both Maximilian's and Rudolph's reigns, and who has been described by a modern scholar, Gottesdiener, as 'the first Jew in Ashkenaz to concern himself with professional history'.[19] He refers to matters of attitude and gesture in relations between Maximilian and the Jews. For him, the Emperor had a positive 'love' for the Jews, and Gans records the visit made by Maximilian, his Empress and court, to the *Judenstadt*, the Prague Jewish quarter, in 1571. Such a thing had indeed not been seen since James I of Aragon visited the Barcelona synagogue in state in 1263. However, it was under Rudolph II after 1576 that the newly-improved condition of Bohemian Jewry received further regularization and development. In 1577, Rudolph issued a charter for Bohemian Jews, which, although it did not allow them to return to the royal towns, explicitly promised that they would never again be expelled from Prague itself, or from the kingdom as a whole. In economic and social terms, Rudolph's charter opened up many new opportunities for Prague's Jews to practise previously forbidden crafts such as jewellery, and gold- and silver-smithing. Thus the traditional Christian guild monopolies were broken up, and the expansion of the Prague Jewish community became possible. Many merchants, artisans, and shopkeepers were now added to the traditional moneylenders, pawnbrokers, and pedlars, and there was a strong upsurge of population. By 1600, the Prague community had grown from its low point of a few dozen in 1564 to over 3,000, and within about forty years of Rudolph's charter the city had surpassed even Amsterdam to become the largest urban Jewry outside the Ottoman Empire, apart from Rome. This expansion, undoubtedly fomented deliberately by Imperial policy, was highly significant in terms of European Jewish history as a whole.[20]

In these circumstances, it is not surprising that the famous leader of the Prague community, Rabbi Judah Löw ben Bezalel, generally known by his rabbinical name, the Maharal, should have said, in a sermon in Poznan in 1592, 'While the ancients fulfilled the Torah under dire poverty, and under persecution of the Gentiles, now we sit in our homes, each one relaxed.'[21] Such economic and social opportunities had scarcely been available anywhere to Jews, since the decline of the medieval Spanish community. It is therefore necessary to examine the likely reasons for this dramatic change in Jewish fortune, in a comparatively unlikely spot, compared with famous and fairly open economic centres of the period, such as Amsterdam and Venice, and one which was to have such an effect on events in the seventeenth century.

Recent scholarship concerning the reigns of Maximilian and more particularly Rudolph, has stressed the central role of religion in determining their policy as a whole, and not simply that towards the Jews. Thus Israel refers to Maximilian's 'lack of religious militancy', and describes him as having been 'throughout his life torn by the relentless religious conflicts and doubts of his time', while he sees Rudolph's court at Prague as 'a key cultural manifestation of the late sixteenth century', whose 'flavour differed markedly from the Catholic and Protestant militancy which reigned officially elsewhere'.[22] Rudolph seems to have taken his positive view of Judaism much further than his father had done, but attitudes must be connected also with the religious situation of the time, both in Bohemia and Moravia and in Austria, where small Jewish communities had been allowed to return to Vienna and Innsbruck. In both countries, Protestantism appeared to be defeating the Catholicism which emperors were required to uphold. For Israel, this situation indicated 'an inescapable need to transcend the Catholic–Protestant conflict', so that Rudolph's actions had political and economic motives, as well as resulting in part from his cultural and religious interest in Judaism, which led in 1592 to his summoning the Maharal for an interview. In Gans's words, which seem, in the scripturally dominated style beloved of earlier, medieval Jewish writers, to be redolent with the encounters between Moses and the Lord,

The great and meritorious luminary, our master the Emperor Rudolph . . . summoned him and gave him a warm and gracious welcome and spoke with him face to face as a man speaks with his neighbour, but the substance and manner of their words are closed, sealed and hidden.[23]

It is very probable that the two were discussing the interests in esoteric matters which they shared. The significance of these for the cultural as well as the general social life of Jews around the year 1600 will be considered in the next chapter, but at this stage it is necessary to examine further the pro-Jewish policy of Maximilian and Rudolph. R. J. W. Evans has stressed, in his work on the Habsburg monarchy in this period, both the importance of religion as a factor in Imperial policy-making and the practical situation in which room was found for Jews to live and, increasingly, flourish. In his view, Austria, Bohemia and the other 'Austrian' lands were in a state of religious apathy, rather than Reformation fervour. Thus to call them 'Protestant' 'indicates what religion was *not*' rather than implying a positive belief, let alone practice. In Evans's view,

> The further practical consequence of such variegated patterns of faith was a widespread *de facto* toleration: not a merit of the Reformation, but the very atmosphere in which it operated, tantamount to its lack of any clear focus. 'In affairs of religion everyone does as he pleases, thus something like peace obtains between the parties', observes one censorious Catholic, and the thought is seconded by a Lutheran: 'In Austria there is almost too much liberty in religion, since all those who have been banished from the rest of Germany, for whatever reason, flood to it with impunity.' 'At Prague, that populous and dirty place', noted the Huguenot Prince de Rohan in 1600, 'there is no German sect of which one cannot find some trace.'[24]

It seems fairly clear, therefore, that even without the emperors' positive sympathy with Judaism, there were likely to be opportunities for leading an increasingly successful Jewish life, in the midst of Hussites, Czech Brethren, and Lutheran and Calvinist refugees and sympathizers; but at about the same time, there was what Israel refers to as 'a general revival of Jewish life' in Germany too.

Once again, ethnic and religious confusion seems to have created opportunities for Jews to move westwards once more. The most conspicuous case is Frankfurt. The community there had shrunk to only 130 by 1500, and the authorities allowed only a few refugees from other places to settle there in the early sixteenth-century expulsion period, so that the population of the ghetto in 1542 was still only 419. However, a rapid expansion, well beyond the rate of increase of the rest of the population, began in the 1570s. As in Prague, some restrictions on Jews' economic activities were removed, and by 1613 nearly 3,000 out of Frankfurt's 20,000 population were Jews. In Israel's view what seems to have happened is that the arrival of Dutch Calvinist immigrants in the 1570s had the effect of breaking up, somewhat, the traditional guild structure, and thus inadvertently assisted the Jews. Once again, external circumstances had fortuitously acted to their advantage, and some Jewish merchants were able to take part in the distribution in south Germany of goods from the Low Countries. At the same time, the ecclesiastical princes, recovering their nerve after the Lutheran onslaught and now feeling strong enough to face down their populations, began to invite Jews back and improve the conditions of Jewish life where communities had survived. Hildesheim, for instance, recalled its Jewry on episcopal initiative in 1577, and soon became one of the largest north German communities, with about thirty families in the town and a dozen more in the surrounding countryside by 1600. When the bishop of Hildesheim became archbishop-elector of Cologne, he pursued the same policy and allowed Jewish resettlement in the 1580s in Hallenberg, Geseke, Werl, and Rüthen. Following the same pattern of anti-Lutheran and pro-Jewish policy, the bishop of Bamberg and the margrave of Ansbach, as joint lords, developed a new and important Jewish community at Fürth, near the Protestant Imperial free city of Nuremberg. Both lords and Jews were thus able to profit from the revived trade route between north Germany and Venice. By 1600, Fürth had become the main Jewish community on the major routes from Frankfurt to Prague and Vienna. In addition, again as a result of lords pursuing their economic interest, the 1570s and 1580s saw Jewish settlement on the north German coast, from which they had previously been largely excluded by the protectionism of the Hansa, or else been expelled along with other Netherlands Jews in the fifteenth century. However, the count of East Friesland now encouraged settlement in Emden and Aurich, thus apparently replacing with Westphalian Jews the Dutch refugees who had returned to their homes at the end of the Duke of Alba's regime. In addition, in 1584, Count Adolf XII of Holstein-Schauenberg allowed a settlement of Jews in his port of Altona outside Hamburg, and even the city itself allowed in some 'Portuguese' to settle and trade in 1590, though still maintaining its traditional exclusion of German Jews. In the seventeenth century, Hamburg came to possess the second most important Sephardic community, after Amsterdam. Faced with such an expansion of Jewish life in Germany, the country's communities began in 1582 to restore a national organization, such as had not existed since the fourteenth century. Western Jewry was reviving.

The 'Portuguese' also began to spread in north Germany, beyond the initial settlement in Hamburg. In the south, they were less welcome as competitors on well-established trade routes, but on the north coast they were useful suppliers of mercantile skills and capital, for example in Emden, Stade, west of Hamburg, and the town of Glückstadt ('Happytown' – misnamed in the view of Jewish wags), founded by Christian IV of Denmark in Holstein, about forty miles down-river from Hamburg. Ashkenazi Jewries, on the other hand, did increase in Frankfurt and other places, though the increased number of centres now willing to receive Jews seems to have reduced the rate of growth of the more established communities. Thus Frankfurt Jewry seems to have trebled in size between 1570 and 1600, but between that year and 1620 it only grew from about 2,500 to less than 3,000. The growth of Jewish life in Germany in this period seems to have depended very much, as in the medieval period, on the initiative of the governing authorities. Christian subjects did not always accept the situation with equanimity, however, and particularly severe riots took place in and around Frankfurt in 1614–15. Trouble had begun in 1612, when the former economic scapegoats of the local guilds, the Dutch Calvinist refugees, had returned to their native land, and all discontent might be focused on the Jews. In 1612, the cloth guilds, led by

Vincent Fettmilch, reprinted Luther's tract *On the Jews and Their Lies*, and used it to stir up the cloth-workers to blame the decline of their industry, in fact due to increasingly effective Dutch and English competition, on the Jewish community. Although the Emperor Matthias tried to mediate, on 22 August 1614 Fettmilch and his henchmen managed to induce an apparently spontaneous working-class rebellion against the ruling patricians, very much as Salvestro dei Medici and his friends had done with the Ciompi uprising in Florence in 1378. However, on this occasion, the breakdown of political authority and public order was exploited to attack the Jewish ghetto. Eventually, the mob broke in and a traditional type of attack took place, in which looting prevailed over violence against people. Israel claims that the lack of Jewish deaths, only two murders being recorded, shows that 'times had indeed changed since the massacres of the fourteenth and fifteenth centuries'.[25] This may be true of certain places in Germany, but the analogy between the Frankfurt uprising of 1614 and the anti-Jewish attacks in Spain in 1391, as well as the anti-*converso* violence in Toledo in 1449 and Córdoba in 1473, seems close. In each case, economic rivalry and robbery were major motives, and the deaths of Jews, however tragic, were relatively incidental. In Frankfurt, the authorities acted quickly to restore order, the ringleaders, including Fettmilch, being duly caught and hanged. Like Henry III of Castile in the late 1390s, the Emperor Matthias ensured that the old government was restored in this 'free' city, and that the Jews were compensated for their losses. The difference, in the new climate of the seventeenth century, was that as a result of the violence the Jews actually received greater privileges and more Imperial protection, to the detriment of the powers of the local authorities.

The Thirty Years War, between 1618 and 1648, could not fail to affect the newly arrived German Jewries, as it did political relations between Jews and Gentiles elsewhere in the vast area of combat, and indeed between the Gentile populations themselves. The progress made in the late sixteenth century had still left Jews excluded from most of the larger states of the Empire, only Bohemia and Hesse being exceptions. In addition, among the Imperial free cities, only Frankfurt allowed Jews to settle, while Hamburg allowed in the 'Portuguese'. It did not seem likely that Ferdinand II, who reigned between 1619 and 1637, would be even more favourable to the Jews than his predecessors, Maximilian II and Rudolph II. However, it appears that the exigencies of war overcame the influence of the Counter-Reformation, which had led to a revival of medieval policies towards Jews in Italy. There is no doubt that some Jewish merchants and financiers did well out of the war. They were able to exploit the needs of Gentile armies of varying nationalities and religious persuasions, thus obtaining benefits, not only for themselves but also for the less fortunate members of their community. The crucial factor, in the early stages of the war, was the traditional link between Jewish communities and the Emperor. He benefited most from their loans, as Jews could be repaid in privileges and concessions which were useful to them. Christian financiers, on the other hand, would only be satisfied with cash. However, it has to be asked whether the success of individual financiers and suppliers, such as Jacob Bassevi, a 'Court Jew' of Prague who was eventually ennobled by the Emperor Matthias, was reflected in the lives of the wider community. In some cases, it is clear that it was, as the Prague *Judenstadt*, for example, was extended in the 1620s, and Bohemian Jews in general were allowed to expand their activities in the grain and wine trades after 1623. In Vienna, Ferdinand rewarded his Jewish supporters with an entirely new *Judenstadt*, free of the control of the municipal council, in Leopoldstadt, including, for the first time in the city since 1421, a synagogue. There were 2,000 Jews in Vienna by 1650. In the 1620s, the Emperor's protection of Jews continued to be effective, for example in Prague, where only the Jewish quarter escaped pillaging in 1620 after the defeat of the Protestants in the battle of the White Mountain. It was effective later too in Halberstadt, where the Lutherans had rioted and destroyed a newly built synagogue in 1621, Imperial troops restoring order for Jews as well as Christians. In Frankfurt and Vienna too, Imperial protection seems to have been largely effective, but the Jewish situation was to improve further after the Swedish invasion of the Empire in 1630. In Israel's words, 'That the Swedes, like the Imperialists, generally treated the Jews better than the rest of the population emerges from a good deal of

contemporary evidence.'[26] Here, a revision of traditional historiography seems to be necessary, despite the offence which may
thus be given to Jewish 'assimilationists'. Paradoxically, the
historians of the Nazi period seem to have been nearer the mark
when they stressed the particular favour shown to Jews by the
Swedes. It appears that, where Swedish control was strong, most
Jews benefited. Settlements were allowed to expand, even
against the wishes of the local authorities, as for example in
Minden where there were apparently twenty or twenty-five
families at the end of the war, compared with the statutory limit
of five, fixed since the 1590s. Once again, economic and military
demands seem to have overcome any anti-Jewish feelings which
Swedes may have possessed, if only in an abstract sense, given
their previous lack of contact with living Jews.

Poland

As has already been observed, Poland, with neighbouring
Lithuania and the Ottoman-ruled territories of the Balkans,
became in the sixteenth century the main centre of Jewish life in
the world, largely as a result of the western European expulsions
of the period between 1470 and 1520. It is essential, therefore, to
consider the nature of that life in Poland and Lithuania.
However, as in the case of Germany and particularly of Luther,
subsequent events significantly obtrude into any attempt to
examine seriously the history of Polish Jews in the early modern
period. As the most superficial reading of Polish history will
show, even such basic matters as the country's territorial bound-
aries have never been uncontroversial, and the whole question of
Poland's national identity has been particularly subject to outside pressure in the period since 1700. Indeed, by 1800, the
ancient kingdom of Poland, which in the early modern period
was combined with the grand duchy of Lithuania in a dual
'Commonwealth', had been cut to pieces by the neighbouring
powers, Austria, Prussia, and Russia. An independent Poland
was reconstituted, again as a result of outside intervention, at
Versailles in 1919. Since then, a short-lived political independence has been shattered and the country radically redesigned,
both geographically and culturally, by the succeeding violent

shocks of intervention by Hitler's Germany and Stalin's Soviet Union. It is hardly plausible to maintain that the mighty Polish Jewish community, which, by the end of the seventeenth century, had probably contained as many as three-quarters of the world's Jews, could have remained untouched and unaffected by these upheavals. In the event, of course, it nearly vanished altogether in the years of Nazi rule, which some saw as the apocalyptic development of the historic anti-Judaism, shading into anti-Semitism, of the Polish state in its independent years. It is perhaps in modern Polish historians, writing both inside and outside the country, that the uneasiness and unhappiness of those who experienced, or have subsequently to contemplate, the history of that country become most apparent. When it comes to the question of the Polish Jews, guilt is added to that uneasiness and unhappiness, whether it concerns the independent Poland of 1919–39, or the Nazi period, or the Communist governments which have been in control since. Whatever the political and historical viewpoint of the writer, the Jews seem to be something of an embarrassment to the non-Jew. There seems to be an underlying feeling that they have been badly treated, but that to indicate this clearly is to admit something which threatens to destroy whatever self-respect and independence, at least of mind, remain to a proud but much-abused people. A case in point is a collection of essays by Polish historians, working both inside and outside the country, which was published in 1982.[27] In this work, Antoni Maczak, for instance, only mentions the Jews of Poland–Lithuania once, in passing, in his discussion of 'estate' theory and practice in the early modern period, despite the fact that they actually formed one of those estates in their own right.[28] In cultural matters, Poland's Jews are completely dismissed as contributors to the life of the country as a whole. 'From the sixteenth century and increasingly through the next two hundred years, Jews became very numerous in the Commonwealth, but Jewish society represented a closed group almost entirely isolated from the mainstream of culture and customs in Poland.'[29]

The essay by Andrzej Wyrobisz, from which this passage is quoted, discusses 'social prestige', so the conclusion of the author seems to be that the Jews, despite their important numerical and economic contribution to that society, had little or none.

This attitude, on the part of at least some modern Polish historians, raises questions of great interest and importance concerning Polish Jewry. In earlier chapters it has been seen that, in western and central Europe in the late medieval and early modern periods, certain factors were always important in determining the ability of Jews to live successfully in different societies and have easy social relations with their Christian neighbours. The first of these factors was the attitude of the governing authorities, without whose approval and legal and political protection Jews could not live anywhere under Christian rule. The second is the extent to which Jews were allowed, within that legal and corporate situation, to diversify their economic activity. If Jews were confined, for example, to the provision of finance, and the services required for the survival of their own communities, then they were indeed likely to be unpopular with the majority population, and largely marginalized in social terms. If, on the other hand, they were allowed to engage in a wide range of economic pursuits, then their social contacts with the Gentiles would become much more elaborate and diverse. Up until about 1500, as a general rule, the social and economic profiles of Jewish communities in northern Europe tended to conform to the former pattern, while those around the Mediterranean corresponded more to the latter. Given that, after 1500, the Polish community came to replace that of Spain as the largest and most important in Europe, it will be necessary to consider whether the judgement of some modern Polish scholars reflects reality – or, in other words, whether such a large and economically and culturally significant part of Jewry could really have lived in the midst of Poles and Lithuanians, and yet have had so little effect upon them. In the process it may be advisable, while exercising due caution in the matter of comparisons, to keep in mind the earlier example of Spain.

Fortunately, there is help to be found in the work of other specialists, both Polish and foreign, who are indeed attempting to appreciate the Jews' proper place in Polish history, in order, in the words of the editors of a recent collection of papers, 'to deny to the Nazis success in their bid to destroy the record of Jewish activity in Europe and, in particular, Poland'.[30] Many scholars, including, recently, Bronislaw Geremek, have considered that between the twelfth and the fifteenth centuries in what gradually became the early modern kingdom of Poland, Jews were one among a number of immigrant groups which influenced the existing population, at all social levels, in its language and customs. In the development of mercantile and artisan communities in Polish territory, the activity of Jews closely paralleled that of the French-speaking Flemings, or Walloons, which suggests that at this stage they did not have a unique economic role, even though they were primarily urban rather than rural inhabitants. Both groups were, however, much less significant numerically than the immigrant Germans.[31] According to Benedykt Zientara, this relative openness to foreigners remained a feature of Poland in the fourteenth and fifteenth centuries. 'Regardless of the xenophobic outbursts which occasionally emerged . . . Poland continued to be a country open to foreign influence and well disposed towards foreigners who brought cultural and technical innovations with them.'[32] However, Aleksander Gieysztor has since put the history of Jews in Poland in a different perspective, in a comprehensive survey of the early modern period, by showing that there were in fact small but important Jewish communities in Poland long before then.

> The presence of Jews in Polish lands before the thirteenth century and their participation in the economic life of old Poland is a phenomenon apparent from both written and other sources. Doubts expressed even by well-known academic authorities on this subject may be disregarded.

The Jewish communities of the region appear to have been Slavonic-speaking up to the eleventh and twelfth centuries, and to have been forced, along with the other inhabitants of these territories, to change their patterns of social and economic life in response to the rapid developments taking place in western Europe in the same period.[33] Thus it is clear that Jews took part, as existing inhabitants of the land, in the general thirteenth-century regularizing of legal status and relations in Poland, when town corporations were set up. The General Charter of Boleslaw the Pious of Cracow, granted in 1264, allowed Jews to travel freely round the country without molestation, to engage in trade, to practise a full religious life, including synagogue worship, ritual burial, and dietary laws, and to be exempt from serfdom and slavery. They were not granted the right to live in towns, or to have the same privileges as autonomous Christian burghers, but Boleslaw's charter, as reissued and confirmed by Kazimierz the Great in 1334, proved to be the basis of the legal status of Jews in Poland until as late as the eighteenth century, despite the fact that no Polish charter was deemed to be valid unless it was confirmed by each succeeding king or noble.

Although Poland did not itself suffer from the fourteenth-century Black Death, it did receive refugees, including Jews, from Germany. After 1400, the Jewish communities were of such significance in the new union with Lithuania that they actually formed an 'estate' of their own, alongside those of clergy, burghers, and peasants. The result of this development seems, however, to have been what Norman Davies calls an 'ossification' of social structures, each estate having its own rights and rules set down in detailed legislation, its membership being determined by birth. In this way, the organization of Jewish communities came very much to parallel that of the other estates, though it should also be pointed out that similar charters were issued to national and ethnic minorities, including the Jewish 'fundamentalist' Karaite sect, Armenians, Tartars, and Scots, and might also be granted, in certain circumstances, to individuals. In the case of the Jews, some privileges were general for all communities, while others covered specific regions or communities. In royal towns, they were issued by the king, or by the *starosta* or governor on his behalf, while in nobles' (*szlachta*) towns, they were granted by the hereditary owners. Each Jewish community had leaders who were determined to enforce internal discipline over its members, and any attempts at innovation involved escape into areas where legal and guild restrictions had no force. Thus, like the oligarchies of the Christian towns, the Jewish *kahal* or *kehilla*, the community as represented by its council, attempted to prevent Jewish artisans from forming guilds of their own, outside the control of the local leadership.[34] It is clear, then, that by 1500 Jews had a significant and well-established place in Poland and Lithuania. Estimates of their numerical strength range from 20,000 to 30,000, divided among about fifty communities in Poland and four in Lithuania.

The first aspect of early modern Jewry in the Commonwealth which needs to be considered is that of demographic growth and composition. Overall, it appears that, between 1500 and 1575, the Jewish population grew to somewhere between 100,000 and 150,000, out of a total for Poland–Lithuania of about seven millions. This clearly constituted the largest Jewish community in Europe in the period, and the question is how far the growth was generated by the existing Jewish inhabitants, and how far it was the result of immigration. In the period up to 1575, it appears that the main cause of expansion was immigration from the west. The local expulsions from Bohemia and Hungary, the latter being aggravated by the partition of the country after 1526 into Habsburg, Ottoman, and Transylvanian sections, meant that most Jewish immigrants to Poland from then on came from Czech or Hungarian areas and, as a result, the number of communities had already greatly expanded by 1560. There were now about 52 in Greater Poland and Masovia, 41 in Little Poland, and 80 in Red Russia, Volhynia, and Podolia, making 173 in the Polish Crown, with an additional 20 in the grand duchy of Lithuania. How exactly this expansion took place is virtually impossible to determine, owing to the lack of useful tax records before 1549. In that year a general capitation tax was levied, enabling Stanislaw Lipnicki, a courtier, to make a census of Jews in Sandomierz, Red Russia, Podolia, Lublin, and Betz. Thereafter, information of a somewhat vague kind becomes available in the censuses of the 1560s and 1570s. However, Baron rightly opposes a defeatist approach to the evidence, despite the catastrophic loss of documentation, for this as for other periods, which resulted from the Holocaust.

A useful case from the mid-sixteenth century is that of Poznán, where it is possible to establish, for some years, the number of houses occupied by Jews. The 1550 and 1552 censuses show, on this basis, that there were about 1,000 Jews in the town, a figure similar to those for Cracow, Lublin, and Lwow, though officially they occupied only forty-nine houses. It does seem that the population density among Jews was much higher than that among Christians, but by 1558 the expansion of the community in Poznán had been acknowledged by the authorities with permission to occupy eighty-three houses, rising to 138 after 1600. It is clear that Jews had found accommodation outside the city walls, as well as within, so that a ghetto, as such, did not exist. In the last decades of the sixteenth century, Jews followed Poles into territories to the east, such as the Baltic areas of Courland, Latvia, and Estonia (where they remained after the Poles withdrew), Pomerania, and the Ukraine. Here, under the Jagiellonian monarchs Bathory and Sigismund III, the Polish Crown was trying to exploit a power-vacuum left by the end of the medieval Russian state based on Kiev, and the continuing threat of the Mongols and Tartars. Polish aristocrats, together with colonists of varied ethnic origin, moved in and settled, allowing Jews an important economic role. After 1570, therefore, the growth of the Polish–Lithuanian Jewish population came to depend more on expansion generated by the existing community than on immigration. By the early seventeenth century, in fact, there was a growing feeling, among the Christian population, that the Jews were breeding frighteningly fast. The contemporary writer, Sebastyan Miczynski (quoted by Baron), tried to provide a satisfactory explanation of this supposed social problem. The Jews, he said, 'hide their total number, even though they multiply enormously, for they do not die in wars, they run away before the "air" [plague] and marry very early'. On the face of it, there might seem to be some plausibility in these suggestions. Jews, like everyone else, would wish to hide from census-takers, whose purpose was to provide statistics for royal tax-collection, and perhaps the confusion of the heavily overcrowded Jewish areas may have helped some individuals to avoid identification.

It is also true that Jews were not allowed to do military service, but it was soon to become clear that civilian status was no guarantee of safety in war. The accusation that Jews, in some way, had special knowledge of disease and were therefore able to avoid it had been conventional in late medieval Europe and caused particular damage to German Jewries in the period of the Black Death. It is perhaps unsurprising that it should have resurfaced in Poland around the year 1600. Finally, Baron has struggled to find reasons for a possible lower mortality rate among Jews than among Christians to match the probability that Jews did indeed marry earlier than their Christian equivalents, and therefore had at least the chance of producing larger families through making more use of the women's period of greatest fertility. Such factors cannot, of course, be quantified, but it does appear that the ratio of Jews to the total population in the Commonwealth, allowing for the expansion of the territory itself in the period concerned, was 0.6 per cent in 1500, 2 per cent in 1576, and 4.5 per cent in 1648, the numbers being about 30,000 in 1500, 150,000 in 1576, and 450,000 in 1648. Baron points out that the rapidity of population growth in the earlier period up to 1576 may have been caused not only by the actual influx of immigrants, but perhaps also by the common feature of immigrant groups that such populations tend to concentrate abnormally in the most reproductive age range, between fifteen and forty-five. Some rates of increase were certainly high, whatever the cause. Volhynia's Jewish population, for example, increased by 500 per cent from 3,000 to 15,000, between 1569 and 1648, and there was a similar rate of increase in Podolia in the same period. In a few cases it is also possible to assess the relative population densities of the Jewish and Christian populations. It appears that, in this period, the average number of people in each household was about five or six, but a Jewish house, as the Poznán example has already suggested, could contain as many as thirteen to twenty-two. It is virtually impossible to check Miczynski's observation on the Jewish ability to avoid death by plague. However, there are available records for the Jewish burial society in Cracow, which show that 1,750 were buried between 1543 and 1600, and no fewer than 2,850 between 1600 and 1650, though it is impossible to discern the causes of the increase from these basic figures.[35] The last question to be considered is that of the losses suffered by the Jewish communities in the Commonwealth as a result of the massacres of 1648 and later, which are normally known by the name of the Ukrainian leader, Chmielnicky, who was responsible for the first attacks. According to Davies's estimate, 56,000 Jews were killed between 1648 and 1656, while a further 30,000 or so also died, as a result of natural causes, flight, or destitution. To what extent these communities recovered after 1660 is a matter for later consideration.

It is clear from the foregoing that the late medieval basis of Jewry in Poland consisted of the protection and privileges granted by the Crown or the nobility, and the possibility of economic activity in the towns. There were, however, limitations on the admission of Jews to urban areas. In Gdańsk and elsewhere on the Baltic coast, for example, including Courland and Livonia, the Lutheran bourgeoisie reduced the opportunity for Jewish immigration, when the refugees started moving eastwards, though the complex local residence regulations did allow a small, transient Jewish population. There were more Jews in the fairly well-established towns of western and central Poland in the early sixteenth century. In other places though, such as Warsaw, Toruń, and Kielce, the local authorities had succeeded in obtaining from the Crown privileges of *Non tolerandis Judaeis* ('Not tolerating Jews'), which were intended to keep the Jews out, but which in fact often contained concessions, such as allowing Jews to enter on market and fair days, as in Toruń, Gdańsk, and Wrociaw.[36] Elsewhere, for example in Poznán and Cracow, the Christian merchants and artisans had sufficient economic muscle to exclude Jewish competition without recourse to the Crown. The towns rarely, if ever, acted together, though, and where the Crown's influence was sufficiently strong, Jewish self-government developed under royal patronage in a manner similar to that elsewhere in Europe. In the late Middle Ages kings had commonly appointed the chief rabbis of Poland and Lithuania, but by the time of Sigismund I, after 1515, the elected leaders of each Jewish *kahal* were permitted to run its internal affairs, under the supervision of the local royal official, the *wojewoda* or *starosta*. In 1530 the Jews were allowed to set up their own legal tribunal at Lublin and in 1549 they were permitted to assess and collect their part of the poll-tax (*pogłówne*), thus inadvertently providing some of the demographic information already referred to. A set of negotiations which took place in Cracow in 1564 shows how *kahal* leaders were able to bargain with the Crown over finance. It would be wrong to suppose, however, that the royal officials did not have a strong position in such discussions. The contemporary source states that, 'These same Jews declared that in many places they were charged excessive tolls, even for individual persons or for empty carts, which was contrary to custom and to their rights and privileges. They begged to be freed from these impositions.'[37] The Crown was hardly in a position to end such abuses, and used the opportunity of negotiating the rate of the poll-tax, which the community leaders would then have to collect, to make further demands – in this case for payments on the Jews' abattoirs and other market activities. But at least the Jews had some forum for the expression of their grievances. In addition, they were, of course, able to follow the example of other estates, and lower their poll-tax contributions by concealing some of their potential taxpayers. As Sigismund II August is said to have remarked to the bishop of Cracow in the mid-sixteenth century, 'Tell me, my lord bishop, since you do not believe in sorcery, how is it that only 16,598 Jews pay the poll-tax, while two hundred thousand of them apparently live underground?'[38]

None the less, whatever efforts the Polish Crown might have made, deliberately or inadvertently, to assist the development of a flourishing Jewish life in Poland and, after 1569, the dual Commonwealth of Poland–Lithuania, the rulers' contribution was always considerably less significant than that of the nobility. After a new constitution was adopted by the Diet in 1539, the influence of the owners of private towns increased, and from that year onwards such owners had the exclusive right to exercise jurisdiction over their Jewish communities – a prerogative which had previously belonged to the royal *wojewodes* – and to place obligations upon their Jewish inhabitants. The severing of the link between the Jews and royal justice, access to which had previously been their unique privilege among the inhabitants of seigneurial towns, should, in Goldberg's view, be seen as part of the growing effort of the lesser Polish nobles, or *szlachta*, to expand their influence at the expense of the Crown. Thus it was in the period after 1539 that Jewish leaders increased their efforts to acquire specifically community, rather than general, privileges. They were simply recognizing the changed political and social situation, which was also clearly understood by the *starostas* in the royal towns, who were generally magnates or lesser nobles themselves. They too began to issue local charters to Jewish communities, especially after 1568.[39]

It was in the economically less developed eastern areas of Polish territory, where nobles were largely in control, that Jews found their greatest opportunities to settle in large numbers and prosper. East of Lublin and Lwow, a Jewish bourgeoisie, with little or no Polish or German competition, succeeded in dominating the main export trades of grain and timber, providing manpower and practical and business skills. All this would not have been possible without the massive support of magnate families, such as the Radziwiłł, Lubormiski, Ostrogorski, Sobieski, and Zamojski, who used the Jews to develop their lands economically. Small Jewish settlements mushroomed, and the Zamojski even imported Spanish-speaking Sephardim (an exotic phenomenon indeed on the borders of Poland and Russia) to assist with the task. The nobles' policy towards the Jews, like that of the royal authorities, was full of ambiguities. Even in royal towns, official hostility towards Jews, while far from disappearing, became less general during the seventeenth century, owing in part to an overall decline of population and hence an increased dependence on Jewish traders. Competition between the traders themselves, Christian and Jewish, inevitably became even more fierce as a result. In private towns, however, the reduction of restrictions on Jews was more pronounced, especially after 1660, though there was still a fear that Jews would 'get ahead of Christians', in particular by meeting the peasants' carts, laden with produce, before they reached the officially controlled markets.[40]

The 'estates' system, which dominated legislation and official thinking from at least the fourteenth century onwards, clearly derived from the traditional tripartite division between clergy, nobles, and peasants. However, the contemporary perception of the breakdown of Polish society, as revealed in the poll-tax assessment of 1520, was very much more complex. The main social categories recognized in this source, each with its own level of contribution per head, were six: clergy, royal officials, nobles, peasants, burghers, and Jews. In addition all these main headings, except significantly that of the Jews, were subdivided, so that for example university scholars and students were regarded as dependents of the clergy, and rural millers and tavern-keepers were included with the peasantry. There are three main ways, therefore, in which early modern Polish society has been studied in recent times. The simple method is to accept contemporary categories at face value. One alternative noted by Davies is to replace the estate-based divisions with tax-brackets, a method which he attempts on the basis of the 1590 poll-tax assessment, as studied by Wyczánski. The results certainly differ from the outline based on 'estates' thinking, separating, for example, the bishops from the rest of the clergy, who find themselves, according to the new system, in five different brackets, according to wealth. However, Davies rejects this as an effective approach. 'For analysts who believe economic relationships to be the driving force of social life, it is absolutely vital. It has the disadvantage of being essentially unhistorical.' While this statement presumably means that sixteenth-century Poles would not have recognized such a way of describing their society, which is undoubtedly true, this does not in itself invalidate the use of the method in modern studies. Similarly 'unhistorical' concepts such as 'feudalism', or the 'Middle Ages' are, after all, found useful by scholars of many ideological hues. The problem of analysing the role of Jews in early modern Poland is, however, a particular one, and neither of the methods used so far is very helpful. It is impossible to place Jews on the economic scale, because they paid a global sum, in accordance with medieval practice in Poland and elsewhere, and were, as has already been noted, assessed by their own community leaders. 'Estates' theory may be slightly more useful, in that it at least reflected social thinking, if not practical reality. Jews were thus judged, in the medieval manner, by their religious affiliation, rather than their economic potency. In legal and social terms, a Jew, in Poland as elsewhere, might only change his estate by means of conversion, at which point his wealth and occupation would begin to affect the decision. Modern concepts of 'social class', as Davies rightly states, have little or no relevance here.[41]

Although the Jews were clearly a 'special case', much of the preceding discussion also applies to those who became their leading supporters, that is, the nobility. Consideration of the Polish aristocracy in this period inevitably raises the question of the character of Polish political society as a whole. The conventional view of the relationship between Crown and aristocracy is stated, for example, by Federowicz. For him, the dual Commonwealth was liable to be viewed by other European rulers as a 'dangerous political experiment', in which 'no king, no matter how charismatic or talented, could ever free himself from his nobility'.

> By the seventeenth century, Polish society had ceased to have any kind of balance of social forces – one social order and one social order alone, had managed to concentrate all political, economic, social and cultural authority into its hand.

Poland had thus become a 'gentry republic', in which nobles *per se* had rights beyond those achieved by any other European aristocracy before the nineteenth century.[42] An alliance with the nobles, should therefore, in principle, have placed the Jews in a fairly unassailable position, from which they could scarcely have been shifted by frustrated burghers, crushed peasants, or even the weak institutions of the Crown. The picture, however, is not so simple. It is quite clear, from the work of both Marxist and non-Marxist historians, that the position of the Polish nobility did greatly strengthen in the late medieval and early modern periods. It was helped by measures extracted from the Crown, such as the Piotrkow statutes of labourers promulgated in 1496, which were aimed at ensuring for the nobles a cheap and steady supply of labour for their estates. This was at the expense, not only of the peasants themselves, but also of the towns, which were no longer to hire short-term, unskilled labourers from the countryside. The process which then followed, often known as the 'second serfdom', had the effect of subjecting large sectors of the rural population to a kind of manorial system, to the benefit of the aristocracy. However, although estates classification did not distinguish, at least for tax-paying purposes, between different levels within the nobility, a transfer to economic categories divides them according to rates of contribution into three – 'senators', or magnates, middle nobles, and petty nobles. As Wyczánski points out, partly as a result of his work on tax evidence, it is clear that 'the nobility in Poland was not a homogeneous class'. From this economic basis, he proceeds to draw political conclusions. In his view, the fact of differences of wealth and economic and social interest within the noble estate gave the kings a chance to retain some room for manoeuvre,

retaining considerable influence up to 1572, though less thereafter. For all but the most wealthy, the main way to power in
sixteenth-century Poland was still to enter royal service.[43]
However, although it is important to bear this background in
mind, when it comes to considering the role of the Jews in this
society, it is necessary to concentrate on the fate of their main
supporters, the magnates.

The value of Jews to the nobles, and especially to the great
lords of the east, was that they could be used to evade the
Christian guild regulations of the towns. They might be
employed as craftsmen and tradesmen by the very guilds whose
regulations they circumvented. Jews acted as moneylenders, inn-
keepers, fences, and brokers, the evidence coming from
municipal regulations which repeatedly forbade them to exercise
these occupations. They also became involved in the grain trade.
The growth in foreign demand for Polish grain in the earlier part
of the sixteenth century provided ample opportunities for both
Jews and Christian burghers, but this trade, which seems never to
have reached more than a single-figure percentage of total production and therefore scarcely qualifies as 'commercial'
agriculture, began to decline once more after 1570. At the same
time, the influence of the upper nobility began to rise, together
with the growth of the new manorial system, and the progressive
takeover by magnates of the assets of the middling nobility. In
the process, the role of Jews increased, as they became the agents
of the newly expanded upper nobility. The successful Jews,
whether craftsmen or merchants, were increasingly enabled by
their new protectors to defeat Christian competition, ignore legal
restrictions and guild regulations, own land, hold tenancies, and
take charge of mortgaged deeds from nobles. The wealthiest
might even, like their earlier equivalents in Spain and Italy, dress
as nobles and copy their lifestyle. Sigismund August attempted
to stop Jews wearing swords and gold chains, but this battle was
lost to the growing influence of the magnates. While the occasional western Jew might have obtained a knighthood, for
example from the duke of Milan in the fifteenth century, Poland
went even further and actually ennobled some individuals. There
are even signs of some Jews claiming not to be liable for taxes, on
the pattern of their patrons.

There was, inevitably, a backlash from the Christian population, which tended to fall indiscriminately on all Jews, rich,
middling, or poor. Whatever disputes there might be between
the guilds, they would always unite against their Jewish competitors, and the attempt by Jews to form guilds of their own would
be used as an excuse to ban them from living in certain towns at
all. There was, however, a marked contrast between Gentile perceptions and the reality of Jewish life. Although Jews attempted,
in many Polish towns, to model their self-governing institutions
on the city councils, operating elaborate systems of electoral
colleges to ensure that 'safe' people were elected, there were
always proportionately fewer electors and enfranchised taxpayers
in the Jewish than in the Gentile community. Noble patronage
might enable Jews to outnumber burghers in a given town, but
most Jews were still outside the 'magic circle' of economic success
and political power. Nevertheless, despite the tastelessness of its
phraseology, in view of twentieth-century events, there is truth
in Davies's remark that, 'Although the pullulating masses of the
ghetto saw little benefit from the activities of their most prosperous confrères, they all shared in the common opprobrium.'[44]
It is clear, then, that late sixteenth- and early seventeenth-
century Poland–Lithuania saw a comparatively diversified Jewish
community evolve, partly under royal, but mainly under noble,
protection. It remains to enquire what, if any, was the effect of
the religious developments of the period on the conditions of
Jewish life in the dual Commonwealth.

It would be wrong, however, to see Christian–Jewish relations
only in legal or economic terms. Hundert has argued that, at least
up to the nineteenth century, it is necessary to describe the dealings between Jews and the other inhabitants of the Polish territories precisely in religious terms. Such categories were of vital
importance in defining the status and social possibilities of Jews
in the Commonwealth. A 'notorious and rather ridiculous law'
of 1643 enunciated three kinds of traders in Poland – Poles,
foreigners, and Jews. However, this representation of the population did not correspond either to the religious or to the social
reality of the period. Discriminatory legislation, whether against
or, on occasions, in favour of Jews, tended to treat them in an
analogous way to other non-Christian groups, such as Tartars

and Turks. When it came to purely business matters, on the other hand, they were normally defined as a 'national' group alongside others such as Armenians, Scots, Italians, and Lithuanians. The tendency was – and unfortunately it is one often imitated by modern scholars – for each side to regard the other as though it were, in Hundert's words, 'an undifferentiated, monolithic group'. Social, economic, and religious relations were all treated in the same way and, as far as religion was concerned, 'the norms of both the church and the synagogue were strongly segregation-ist in their intent, and . . . each faith taught that the other was spiritually and morally inferior'.

However convenient it might be, from the historian's point of view, to separate social and economic relations between Christians and Jews from their religious dealings, the evidence does not allow this to be done. In seventeenth-century Lublin and Belzyce, for instance, Jews might be opposed by the existing Christian merchants because of their competitiveness, but the Jews were, in this context, treated in the same way as other rivals, such as Lithuanians and Scots. In the case of the Jews, however, internal pressures in their own communities also contributed, alongside Gentile restrictions, to the limitation of social contact between adherents of the two religions. Jewish merchants generally travel-led in groups of the same faith, but the scandalized comments of the preacher Sevi Hirsh ben Aaron Samuel Koidonover indicate that individual Jews often found it desirable to melt into the Gentile population when on business, shaving their beards, adopting Christian names and refusing to admit their true faith, frequenting non-Jewish taverns, and breaking dietary laws. Social pressures on individuals to deny their origins had to counter-balance not only religious restrictions on contact with Gentiles but also Jewish law, repeatedly re-enacted by community councils, which prescribed that they should not go into partner-ship with Christian merchants, even on a temporary basis, and that any Jew who betrayed 'the secrets of Israel' to a Christian merchant or nobleman would be subject to a ban, or exclusion from the community. As Hundert comments, 'A Jew who pooled his interests with a Christian defied heaven and the strongest sanctions of his community', yet the very repetition of the Jewish legislation is a strong indication that it was being extensively ignored.

The pressures against Jewish–Christian partnerships in business also came, of course, from the Christian side. A common social attitude was expressed by the seventeenth-century commentator, Sebastian Miczynski, who warned that 'whoever forms partnerships with Jews . . . should know that he will always suffer losses. . . . Betrayal and fraud await you.' In reality, equal partnerships between Jews and Christians were rare. Generally, the Christian would provide funds to enable Jews to work at a secondary economic level, in the elaboration of raw materials or in the distribution of imported goods. Thus, at least up to the early eighteenth century, Jews continued to develop their activities in small-scale domestic commerce. In addition, particularly in the private towns, they played a large though secondary part in international trade. The influence on these developments of the religious changes in the sixteenth- and seventeenth-century Commonwealth was inevitably considerable; but, in order to understand the relationship between the Jews and the so-called 'religious toleration' in Poland during this period, it is necessary first to consider the religious landscape as a whole.[45]

In the first place, it is important to notice that the Jewish community itself was not all of one religious persuasion. Poland's oldest 'unorthodox' sect was that of the Karaites, who had originated in the east in the eighth century and whose main distinguishing characteristic was its adherence to a fundamentalist view of the text of the Hebrew Bible, which involved the rejection of the oral law and rabbinical commentary included in the Talmud. In the thirteenth century it had occasionally seemed to Christians that the Karaites shared with them a common belief, because of their joint opposition to the rabbinical Judaism by which most medieval Jews endeavoured to live. In the sixteenth century some Protestants, perhaps influenced by the Reformers' frequent equation of the Catholic clergy and the New Testament 'Scribes and Pharisees', once again saw potential allies in the Karaites. In Poland, the main Karaite scholar in this period was Isaac ben Abraham of Troki, who certainly had links with some Protestants who rejected the traditional Trinitarian doctrine held in common by Catholics and the leading Reformers. Troki in the mid-sixteenth century was, in Davies's words, 'a natural laboratory for religious cross-fertilisation'. It contained within it not only a Catholic church and a Karaite *kenessah*, or meeting-house, but also a Tartar mosque and a monastery of the Uniate Church, which followed the Orthodox rite but was none the less in communion with Rome. Into this diverse religious scene came, in the 1570s, an anti-Trinitarian group, including some people known as 'uncircumcised Jews', who took up some of the ritual practices of the Mosaic law. The Christian Hebraist, Szymon Budny, arrived in Troki at this time, and Isaac ben Abraham, attentively following Budny's disputes with Czechowicz, struggled to defend what hc saw as Karaite purity against the anti-Trinitarian argument, which, while removing one of the main theological obstacles between Christians and Jews, none the less continued to assert that Jesus was the natural fulfilment of Old Testament prophecy. As Davies shrewdly remarks, 'In its own day, this Polish-Hebrew theological cocktail passed virtually un-noticed in the outside world; but with time it fermented into a mixture of explosive proportions.'[46]

The full diversity of the Polish religious scene is described, however, by Janusz Tazbir. In the early modern period, the Commonwealth contained, in addition to the Catholic Church, members of those churches that were to become the mainstream Reformation churches – Lutherans and Calvinists – as well as supporters of what is generally known as the 'Radical Reformation', such as Socinians, Anabaptists and Mennonites. These latter were allowed asylum in Polish–Lithuanian territory even when they were excluded elsewhere. There was some analogy between this state of affairs and the situation at the time in the Netherlands and in Transylvania, for example. The distinctive feature of the Commonwealth, however, was that it contained other minority sects which dated back to well before the European Reformation, such as the Armenian Monophysites, who denied the human aspect of Christ's nature, seeing him as a purely divine figure; the Czech Brethren or Hussites, whose movement originated in the fifteenth century; and the eastern Orthodox Church. There were also Muslim Tartars in Lithuania. This 'mosaic' of faiths, as Tazbir describes it, managed to survive the pressures, in both the Catholic Counter-Reformation and the various Protestant camps, for greater unity in the face of the 'enemy'. The long-term 'victory' went, of course, to the Catholics

though individual beliefs did not always correspond to an outward Catholic conformity which was seen very much, and not for
the last time in Polish history, as a gesture of national and
cultural solidarity. The question is, whether the Jews succeeded
in benefiting from this variety and fluidity of faiths.

It is clear, to begin with, that the efforts made by the Catholic
Church, especially after the mid-sixteenth century, to regain lost
ground in Poland–Lithuania had the effect of reviving traditional religious and social hostility towards Jews and Judaism.
Moreover, the educational process, particularly after the Jesuits
started working in Poland in the latter part of the century, was
important in inculcating anti-Jewish as well as anti-Protestant
feeling. There were frequent riots and individual attacks on Jews
and Jewish streets. A virulent genre of middle-class anti-Jewish
literature developed, and accusations of ritual murder and host
desecration resurfaced on a large scale. Thus in Cracow, between
1610 and 1700, there were nineteen anti-Jewish (and also anti-
Protestant) riots, and there were four such incidents in Lublin
between 1620 and 1676. In addition, there were seven trials for
'ritual murder', and/or host desecration in Polish lands. In
Hundert's view, the polemicist Sebastian Petrycy, who actually
proposed the expulsion of the Jews from the dual Commonwealth, reflects quite accurately the attitudes of Christian
burghers in the seventeenth century. Not all his views were negative. He admitted that his Jewish compatriots performed useful
services in supplying money to people in need, in paying higher
taxes to the Polish royal treasury, and in being fairly punctilious
in paying tolls and duties on their trade. They also had a reputa-
tion for being peaceful and law-abiding. However, against all
this was, in Petrycy's mind, a complex of social, economic, and
religious accusations for, at the same time as being so public-
spirited, Jews were also said to be blasphemers, host-desecrators,
users of Christian blood, bribers of judges, seducers of Christian
married women and virgins, debasers of coins, hoarders and
illegal exporters of gold, riggers of weights and measures, oppres-
sors of villagers in their role as tax-farmers (*arendars*) and, as merchants, stealers of the livelihood of Christian artisans. Most
serious of all, they enticed Christians away from their faith. Thus
the full battery of medieval anti-Judaism flourished in the

seventeenth-century Polish Commonwealth, but it has to be said that the likes of Sevi Hirsh encouraged their Jewish flock to have a similar attitude towards the Gentile world around them. For the rabbi, the society of non-Jews was full of idolatry, violence, and drunkenness. Christians, lacking divinely taught ethics, were in the process of sliding steadily into chaos, and a Jew could best save his body and soul by avoiding all contact with them. Clearly these mutual prejudices and hostile injunctions were in practice defied by many Christians and Jews, so that the 'invisible wall' between the two communities was only partial. None the less, it appears that Polish Protestant dissent from Catholicism and Polish Judaism largely ignored each other in this period. The debates within Christianity, with the exception of those involving a few figures – such as in Troki – took place without reference to the living adherents of other faiths, and the political and economic development of the country as a whole had the main responsibility for changing the framework in which its Jews sought to live their lives.

Notes

1 Jacques Heers, 'Portugais et Génois au XVe siècle: la rivalité atlantique-méditerranée', *Actas do III Coloquio Internacional de Estudos Luso-Brasileiros*, ii, Lisbon, 1966, pp. 138–47.

2 Zvi Avneri, 'Bayonne', in *Encyclopaedia Judaica*, iv. cols 350–1; Jonathan Israel, *European Jewry in the Age of Mercantilism, 1550–1750*, Oxford, Clarendon Press, 1985, pp. 51–2.

3 I. S. Révah, 'Pour l'histoire des Marranes à Anvers: recensements de la "nation portugaise" de 1571 à 1666', *Révue des Etudes Juives*, cxxii (1963), 123–47.

4 J. A. Goris, *Etude sur les colonies marchandes méridionales (Portugais, Espagnols, Italiens) à Anvers de 1488 à 1567. Contribution à l'histoire des débuts du capitalisme moderne*, Louvain, Louvain University Press, 1925, pp. 54–5; Geoffrey Parker, *The Dutch Revolt*, rev. edn, Harmondsworth, Penguin, 1985, pp. 59–60, 285n.

5 In Révah, 'Pour l'histoire', p. 128.

6 Phyllis Mack Crew, *Calvinist Preaching and Iconoclasm in the Netherlands, 1544–1569*, Cambridge, Cambridge University Press, 1978.

7 Israel, *European Jewry*, p. 259.

8 Henry Kamen, *The Rise of Toleration*, London, Weidenfeld & Nicolson, 1967, p. 7.

9 Crew, *Calvinist Preaching*, pp. 111, 112. For early Reformation attacks on the Catholic clergy, see R. W. Scribner, *For the Sake of Simple Folk*.

Popular Propaganda for the German Reformation, Cambridge, Cambridge University Press, 1981, pp. 37–58.

10　Parker, *Dutch Revolt*, p. 74.

11　ibid., p. 155.

12　R. W. Truman and A. Gordon Kinder, 'The pursuit of Spanish heretics in the Low Countries: the activities of Alonso del Canto, 1561–1564', *Journal of Ecclesiastical History*, xxx (1979), 65–93.

13　Révah, 'Pour l'histoire', p. 128.

14　Israel, *European Jewry*, p. 62.

15　Israel, 'The economic contribution of Dutch Sephardi Jewry to Holland's golden age, 1598–1713', *Tijdschrift voor Geschiedenis*, xcvi (1983), 534.

16　Israel, *European Jewry*, pp. 11–13.

17　ibid., p. 15.

18　ibid., pp. 38–9.

19　Quoted in Lionel Kochan, *The Jew and his History*, London, Macmillan, 1977, p. 42.

20　Israel, *European Jewry*, p. 40.

21　Quoted in Kochan, *The Jew*, p. 43.

22　Israel, *European Jewry*, pp. 39–40.

23　Quoted in Kochan, *The Jew*, p. 45.

24　R. J. W. Evans, *The Making of the Habsburg Monarchy, 1550–1700*, Oxford, Clarendon Press, 1979, pp. 3, 13.

25　Israel, *European Jewry*, p. 69.

26　ibid., p. 95.

27　J. K. Federowicz, Maria Bogucka, Henryk Samsonowicz, eds, *A Republic of Nobles. Studies in Polish History to 1864*, Cambridge, Cambridge University Press, 1982.

28　Antoni Maczak, 'The structure of power in the Commonwealth of the sixteenth and seventeenth centuries', in *A Republic*, pp. 113–34.

29　Andrzej Wyrobisz, 'The arts and social prestige in Poland between the sixteenth and eighteenth centuries', in *A Republic*, p. 176.

30　Chimen Abramsky, Maciej Jachimczyk, Antony Polonsky, eds, *The Jews in Poland*, Oxford, Blackwell, 1986, p. 12.

31　Bronislaw Geremek, 'Poland and the cultural geography of medieval Europe', in *A Republic*, p. 221.

32　Benedykt Zientara, '*Meloratio Terrae*: the thirteenth-century breakthrough in Polish history', in *A Republic*, p. 47.

33　Aleksander Gieysztor, 'The beginnings of Jewish settlement in the Polish lands', in *Jews in Poland*, pp. 15–21.

34　Norman Davies, *God's Playground. A History of Poland in Two Volumes*, i, *The Origins to 1795*, Oxford, Clarendon Press, 1973, pp. 79–80, 96, 126–7; Jacob Goldberg, 'The privileges granted to Jewish communities of the Polish Commonwealth as a stabilising factor in Jewish support', in *Jews in Poland*, pp. 31–54; Gershon David Hundert, 'On the Jewish community in Poland during the seventeenth century: some comparative perspectives', *Révue des Etudes Juives*, cxlii (1983), pp. 349–72.

35 S. W. Baron, *A Social and Religious History of the Jews*, xvi *Poland–Lithuania, 1500–1650*, New York/Philadelphia, Columbia University Press, Jewish Publications Society of America, 1976, pp. 4–9, 15–23, 164–213.

36 G. D. Hundert, 'The implications of Jewish economic activities for Christian–Jewish relations in the Polish Commonwealth', in *Jews in Poland*, p. 58.

37 Davies, *God's Playground*, i, p. 131.

38 ibid., p. 132.

39 Goldberg, 'Privileges', pp. 35–7.

40 Hundert, 'Implications', pp. 58–60.

41 Davies, *God's Playground*, i, pp. 201–7 (diagram on p. 204).

42 Federowicz, introduction to *A Republic* pp. 1–6.

43 Andrzej Wyczánski, 'The problem of authority in sixteenth-century Poland: an essay in reinterpretation', in *A Republic*, pp. 91, 106–8.

44 Davies, *God's Playground*, i, 213, 290, 297–319.

45 Hundert, 'Implications', pp. 55–63.

46 Davies, *God's Playground*, i, pp. 213, 191–2; for the remainder of this chapter, see Janusz Tazbir, 'The fate of Polish Protestantism in the seventeenth century', in *A Republic*, pp. 201–17, esp. pp. 201–2, 217; Hundert, 'Implications', pp. 56–7; see also Tazbir, *A State without Stakes. Polish Religious Toleration in the Sixteenth and Seventeenth centuries*, Warsaw and New York, Twayne, 1973.

5

A 'modern' Jewish life?

As a result of the Jewish experience of assimilation, followed by rejection and even attempted extermination in the nineteenth and
twentieth centuries, it is natural and inevitable that the life of Jews
in the period between 1500 and 1700 will be examined with a view
to determining the extent to which relations between the Jewish
minority and the Christian majority changed. However, it is at
least as important to consider internal Jewish community life in
'Catholic' Europe in those two centuries in order to assess the
effects of the major external changes, discussed elsewhere in this
work, on the life of individual Jews in various countries. The great
'modern' German-Jewish historian of the nineteenth century,
Heinrich Graetz, was clear on the point. 'It is astonishing, and yet
not astonishing, that the surging movement, the convulsive
heaving that shook the Christian world from pole to pole in the
first quarter of the sixteenth century scarcely touched the Jews at
heart.' Rather, the Jews 'needed no new epoch to begin for them'.
Unlike the Gentiles of western and central Europe, 'they needed
no regeneration'.[1] In order to assess the truth of this judgement in
the light of more recent research, it will be necessary to examine in
particular the major Jewish communities in Italy, in Poland, and
in the Netherlands, with a look back to the more important communities of the late medieval period, in Spain, southern France
and, again, Italy. This selective approach is dictated, not only by
historical considerations, but also by the extreme variations in the
surviving evidence, as well as the quality and extent of specialized
research, in different countries and regions.

Although, as has been seen, western European Jewry was in general decline in the late fifteenth century, it none the less left a distinct heritage and a powerful influence to its successors. As Kriegel has written concerning the Mediterranean communities in the late Middle Ages,

> The Jewish communities of Spain and southern France appeared equally to have had an exceptional history: it should have been a happy one. Hence the seductive effect which it exercised in the last century on the Jews who had been newly received into European society, the beneficiaries of a totally new emancipation, who aspired, above all in Germany, to reconcile a full integration into the country which was ready to adopt them, and the desire to preserve a specific identity. They elevated the 'Spanish period' of Jewish history to the rank of a model.[2]

Since the Holocaust, however, the attractions of assimilation have seemed less obvious to many, and the stock of the late medieval Sephardim has fallen. Unease among the descendants of those Jews who thought themselves to be German, as well as those from other parts of Europe who fell victim to German policy, has in many cases caused an inability, or more probably an unwillingness, to understand the desire of late medieval and early modern Jews in southern France, Spain, and Italy to be regarded as full citizens of their local communities and states. In view of the collapse of the Spanish, Portuguese, and French communities, other than some remnants in papal territories, it is necessary to examine the survival of Mediterranean Jewish life as it appeared in Italy.

Even with the generally massive and impressive survival of archive material in the country, much work still remains to be done on the sixteenth- and seventeenth-century Italian communities. In the meantime, Shulvass provides the best general, but detailed, survey. For him, the Italian Renaissance was 'one of the most significant eras in human history', which had the effect of increasing the willingness of rulers to make legal arrangements, *condotte*, with Jewish communities and individuals. Two important phenomena in the history of early modern Jewry in

Italy were the extensive political fragmentation of the country and considerable Jewish immigration from elsewhere in western Europe as a result of expulsion and persecution. The life which the immigrants found among their Italian co-religionaries was secure and relatively assimilated in cultural and artistic terms, compared with that in many of the countries which they had left, other than Spain. However, few Italian Jews in this period seem to have felt the need or desire to convert to Christianity. In Ferrara, for instance, only ninety-four individuals took this step between 1531 and 1600, though a persecution in the kingdom of Naples early in the century, which was largely directed against *conversos*, did produce greater movement towards the Church. Jews lived in most regions of Italy in this period, including Venice, Padua, Verona, and fifty or so other places in the Veneto, Lombardy, Monferrato, the cities of Mantua and Ferrara, Florence, the papal states, where by far the largest population was to be found, the duchy of Urbino, the cities of Reggio and Modena, the duchy of Parma, and Tuscany. Grudgingly, Shulvass has to admit that there were close links between Jews and Christians in Renaissance Italy, and he blames these for what he describes as the weakness of Jewish communal institutions. Even without involvement with Gentiles, the Jewish population contained a mixture of national origins (such as Spanish, German, and Italian), languages – though Italian was the *lingua franca* – and even physical appearance, as has been noted in chapter one. The late medieval and sixteenth-century practice of *condotte* appeared to encourage individual rather than communal activity, though the papal onslaught after about 1550 tended to induce greater social cohesion among Jews, often as a result of legislative pressure, such as the ordinances in Rome in 1524 and Florence in 1571. There was conflict between groups within Jewish communities, for example between the existing inhabitants and Sephardic immigrants, and, on occasions, Gentiles seem to have been more trusted than other Jews. Religious leadership, as in many other earlier Mediterranean communities, needed the support of mercantile and financial leaders in order to function effectively, and many Jews trusted Christian judges enough to place most disputes in their hands. As has already been noted, there was also considerable pressure on

traditional Jewish family life as a result of the extensiveness of
social dealings with Christians. To Shulvass's horror, Jews seem
to have imitated the doubtful morals of other members of
society, including the involvement of both men and women in
prostitution. Inevitably, sexual relations between Jews and
Christians, which were frowned on by the leaders of both communities, are frequently found in the records. In Florence, for
example, 40 per cent of the indictments of Jewish males in this
period were for relations with Christian women, while Jewish
women found lovers, and sometimes even husbands, among
Christians, especially aristocrats. Jews shared in the contemporary 'feminist'–misogynist debate in Italian society at the
literary level, but, in the meantime, Jewish women found an
economic and social role as managers of pawnshops, as traders,
for example at fairs, and even as contractors for the supply of
clothing for the papal troops.

The education of Italian Jews in this period was inevitably
affected by these developments. In contrast with Jews in Spain
and Portugal, small communities often made no arrangements
for the teaching of their young other than the hiring of private
tutors, who were generally under strong humanistic influence
and in many cases actually Christians. According to Rabbi David
ibn Yachia, the core of a Jew's education (and this of course normally meant a male Jew) was still the Talmud, as throughout the
Middle Ages, while such 'secular' or Gentile learning as
grammar, poetics, logic, and philosophy – for example that of
the Muslim Al-Ghazzali – formed the 'dessert'. Serious Jewish
scholars still regarded their main task as being to start with
Maimonides' famous commentary on the Law, the *Mishneh
Torah*, and then move on to the Talmud, beginning with the
Mishnah and continuing with the works of the Tosaphists. This,
at least, is the account given by perhaps the most famous
scholarly figure of early modern Italian Jewry, Leone Modena. An
able boy was hoped or expected to emulate one who, according to
an entry by his proud father in a prayer-book of the period,

At the age of three, . . . knew his creator. Praised be the Lord
that on the first day of Iyar 1560 he began to study. At the age
of 4½ he recited the *haftorah* in synagogue. . . . He started to

write at the age of 5½. At 6½ he, thank God, started to put on *teffillin*. At eight and a month . . . he began the study of Alfasi. . . . At 12½ he started to read Torah in the synagogue.

The less able seem to have learned by heart primers of Jewish devotion such as that composed by Rabbi Abraham Jaghel Gallichi. However, it appears that the typical Jewish education in Italy in this period, at least for the children of the more prosperous, consisted of a mixture of 'Torah and good manners'. The latter apparently involved a mixture of social graces such as singing and dancing, including the full use of contemporary Italian Gentile musical skills and styles, which at the time inspired the fashions of much of Europe. They also included philosophical studies, which owed much to the ancient Greeks and Romans as well as to Christians of subsequent centuries.

In their style and manner of life, sixteenth-century Italian Jews copied their Christian equivalents, according to their social and economic possibilities. They were as likely to own country houses or to indulge in gambling and other vices as their Gentile contemporaries. In general, Shulvass rightly characterizes the relationship between Jews and Christians in Italy in this period as one of 'genuine closeness', such as was shown in the reaction of many Christians to the increasingly repressive legislation which was imposed by Counter-Reformation popes. A police officer in Terni, for example, said to Jewish prisoners from Civitanova, according to a Jewish source who appears to have slightly adjusted the speaker's manner of referring to God,

And I love you all as myself, and I want to treat you well, for the Holy One, blessed be He, has never forsaken you, and you, although in exile, are beloved by God, and He constantly performs miracles and wondrous acts on behalf of the Israelite nation.

Such Gentile respect, and even affection, towards Jews did not, however, deter rabbis from regarding the papal burning of the Talmud in 1553 as an act of divine retribution for what Rabbi Immanuel da Benevento described as 'the sin of those who derided it and the many ignorant who took pride . . . in false opinions . . . and attacked the masters of the Talmud'.[3]

Evidence from Christian sources for such a close relationship between Italian Christians and Jews may be found, for example, in the archives of Venice. In 1576, Noah the Jew was charged with keeping a gaming-house for both Christians and Jews, while four years later, a goldsmith called Domenico reported to the Inquisition that, when he and a colleague were making two 'pyramids', or *rimmonim*, to adorn the scrolls of the Law, he had said to their employer, ' "We don't know who is to be saved – the Jews or we others" and he told the story of the father who gave three rings to his sons, and each of them thought he had the true one'. As Pullan comments, 'It may be that Boccaccio's story [in the *Decameron*] told by Melchizedek the Jew to Soldan Saladin, was as familiar to Antonio [the goldsmith's colleague] as to Domenico Scandella, the miller of Friuli who was to repeat it to the Inquisition in 1599' (see p. 152). In another case, Valeria Brugnaleschi, the Christian widow of a physician, admitted to the inquisitors that, in 1585, she had lived in the ghetto, 'teaching and reading from the Old Testament to some seventy or eighty Jewish girls at a farthing a time, and eating and drinking food which the Jews supplied to her'. This apparently included fish and *matzos* (unleavened bread), but not meat. The Inquisition was mainly worried by Christians who not merely consorted with Jews, even in the ghetto itself, but also showed excessive familiarity with Jewish ceremonies and customs.[4]

In Venice as elsewhere, and above all in Mantua, music provided many opportunities for social relations between Jews and Christians at a higher social and artistic level. According to traditional historiography, the involvement of Jews in music-making according to the developing styles of Christian Italy was the result of the work, in particular, of the composer Solomon Rossi of Mantua and the famous rabbi, Leone Modena. However, in the words of Israel Adler, the music written by Italian Jewish composers for synagogue and other religious and social use by Jews in Padua, Mantua, and Venice, as well as other places, between about 1550 and 1650, was none other than 'a prolongation, a belated illustration, of one of the well-known features of Italian Jewry during the Renaissance: the assimilation of cultural values from the surrounding civilisation'. Music thus had a sound basis in Jewish legal practice (*halakah*), despite the opposition of some Jews to all music in synagogue, an attitude which was amply reflected in some Catholic and Protestant circles in that and later centuries. It appears from rabbinical *responsa* and other literary sources that Leone Modena and others were attempting, in the style later to be followed for example by the Christian preacher John Wesley, to rescue good music from the streets and the taverns, and put it to its rightful, sacred use. Sarfati wrote of his experience in Padua, before 1565, that such a use was 'certainly preferable to those who strike up vulgar songs which are sung in the streets'. However, the most famous statements on this subject come from the distinguished composer of Mantua, Solomon Rossi himself. In 1622, or thereabouts, he wrote,

> Since God opened my ear . . . and has given me the grace to understand and to teach the science of music . . . my soul rejoiced . . . to thank God . . . with song and praise . . . and God was a support to me and he put into my mouth new songs which I have done according to the order . . . for the times of joy and the feasts . . . and always . . . I have multiplied my efforts to make sublime the psalms of David . . . until I had set many of them to music.[5]

Nowhere else in Europe in this period did integration of a cultural or social kind take so complete a form, and this point can best be made by means of a comparison with the most numerous Jewish population in early modern Europe, that of the dual Commonwealth of Poland–Lithuania. It has already been seen that many Jews, to judge from rabbinical protests, did consort with Christian Poles, even to the extent of compromising the practice of their faith. None the less, the most prominent feature of Jewish life in the dual Commonwealth in this period seems to have been devotion to traditional Talmudic study rather than a rapprochement with the newer ideas of Christian society, which had such considerable repercussions in Poland. The assessment of the nature and significance of Jewish religious life in the region in these centuries reveals fascinating differences of approach between two of the leading Jewish historians, Graetz and Baron. For the latter, the period was 'Poland's Golden Age', in which the medieval structure of Jewish communities, with their stress on religious leadership and rabbinically controlled education and charitable institutions – such as those which had provoked the competition of the *Monte di Pietà* movement in Italy – was largely retained and developed. In spiritual terms, this was a period of 'extraordinary creative élan', and the intellectual strength of Polish Jewry did indeed eventually lead to some interest in Christian intellectual ideas which alarmed the rabbinate, just as such developments had done in Spain and Italy since the Middle Ages. Because of the catastrophic loss of many of the records of the Polish communities, it is very hard, if not impossible, to write the 'internal' history of Jews in the late medieval and early modern periods, other than in terms of religious developments. However, Graetz, who could have had access to such records, chose instead to deliver a blistering attack on the rabbinical leadership of the period, which reflects very much a nineteenth-century German perception of the co-religionaries to the east. Thus he refers to 'grey-headed rabbis, with very little knowledge of the Talmud, who behaved impiously to congregations, and to people of real knowledge, excommunicated and re-admitted members, ordained disciples – all for their own selfish purposes'. The result, according to Graetz, was to create a particular kind of Polish male Jew, which he describes in a passage which, as a result of the horrors of the Third Reich, has a far more sinister aspect than the author can possibly have intended. The prominence of Talmudic study meant that, for him,

> the whole tendency of Jewish thought in Poland was turned in a wrong direction. The language of the Jews in particular suffered from this cause, degenerating into a ridiculous jargon, a mixture of German, Polish and Talmudical elements, becoming an unpleasant stammering, rendered still more repulsive by forced attempts at wit. . . . Together with their language, the Polish Jews lost that which really constitutes a man, and were thus exposed to the scorn and contempt of non-Jewish society.[6]

Few will recognize, in this passage, the great achievements of Polish Jewish culture, which undoubtedly developed significantly in the early modern period, and which will be briefly considered in chapter seven.

The third major example of a Jewish community to be examined at this stage is that of Amsterdam, often known, then and since, as the 'Dutch Jerusalem'. The Amsterdam community of the seventeenth century had, in Méchoulan and Nahon's words, 'an importance in Jewish history out of all proportion to its membership', which appears to have been less that 4,000 at its maximum. The late-sixteenth-century community, known as the House of Jacob (*Beth Ya'acob*), acquired a cemetery of its own in 1607, while a year later a group split away to found a second community called The Dwelling-Place of Peace (*Neveh Shalom*). The difficulties under which Jews still lived, despite moves towards religious freedom in the newly independent United Provinces, were discussed in the previous chapter. As far as internal organization and life is concerned, however, the vitality of the Netherlandish communities in this period, in particular that of Amsterdam, is widely recognized. This is due to the intellectual ferment of the seventeenth century (see chapters six and seven), in which the Dutch Jewish leadership became heavily involved.

It was in 1639 that the three Amsterdam communities which then existed – for another group had seceded from *Neveh Shalom* in 1619 to become *Beth Yisrael*, the House of Israel – united to form a single *Talmud Torah* (Teaching of the Law). The new community contained a wide social spectrum, ranging from leading merchants, doctors, manufacturers, and diplomats to indigent poor in need of communal charity. Jewish life around the Joodenbreestraat was a prominent feature of the city, much commented on by foreign visitors for its public and open nature, and it appeared extensively in the works of the master-painter Rembrandt. The language of the Amsterdam Jews, according to their extensive archives, was predominantly Iberian, partly Spanish but mainly Portuguese. This proportion reflected the respective situations of *conversos* in the two Peninsular kingdoms, with far more such individuals with an abiding interest in Judaism among the 'Portuguese'. As the Talmud Torah community indicated with its seal, showing a phoenix rising from the ashes, it saw itself very much as the revival of the great Spanish and Portuguese communities of the Middle Ages. Its proudest moment was the dedication, in 1675, of the splendid 'Portuguese' synagogue. According to its rules, the 'Spanish and

Portuguese' nation was governed by a council, the *ma'amad*, consisting of six *parnassim*, or wardens, and a *gabbai*, or treasurer. This council controlled internal taxation, appointed religious officers, including rabbis and schoolmasters, and attempted to ensure good morals and religious orthodoxy in the community. For this purpose, the weapon of the *herem*, or anathema, was used. Often, this word is translated as 'excommunication', a specifically Christian term for exclusion from the sacraments, or religious acts and ceremonies, of the church or community. In the Jewish case, in Amsterdam as elsewhere in early modern Europe, the anathema might mean anything from exclusion for a few days to permanent expulsion.

The two most prominent features of the Amsterdam community in this period were, firstly, its remarkable retention of its Iberian identity, which allowed *conversos* and their descendants, many of whom had never previously had any direct link with unbaptized Jews to explore the faith, and secondly its educational and cultural activities. As Méchoulan and Nahon comment,

> The intellectual life of the 'Nation' was dominated by one absolute imperative: to teach Judaism anew to immigrants who had, in whole or in part, lost it. As a result, there was an extraordinary blossoming of writing in the vernacular, Spanish or Portuguese, which set out the principles and rites of Judaism, answered the questions of the crypto-Jews whose links with tradition had been abruptly broken, and was intended to counteract the effects of Calvinist proselytism.

The Netherlands were in any case an area with a high quality of education by contemporary standards, with 'Latin schools' and over 3,000 printers already in action. The Dutch *parnassim*, with the financial help of wealthy community members, set up their own parallel education system. In 1637, there was added to the existing schools, which dated back to 1616, a university known as *Ets Haim* (The Tree of Life), which offered bursaries to students of sufficient merit. The curriculum consisted of training in the sacred texts, Hebrew grammar, and the writing of Hebrew poetry. Wealthier families were able to provide their offspring, or at least their sons, with tuition in the art of writing, and in secular disciplines, at home. The Dutch system, and primarily that of Amsterdam, was so successful that it was later copied in Poland.[7]

The question of outside influences on Jewish communities arises in this as in other cases. As far as internal organization is concerned, the large debt of Amsterdam to the experience of Venice was clearly acknowledged. As far as the education system was concerned, there are three possible influences on developments, namely the example of the Dutch Gentile system, the growing and often successful teaching activity of the Jesuits, and a natural and traditional desire within the Jewish community itself to ensure the transmission of knowledge and understanding of the sacred texts which was the main, if not the only, method of survival in the Diaspora. Overall, what appears is a balance between tradition and modern influences. Certain old values remained, and were renewed, as will be seen in later chapters, in matters of religion, but old social attitudes also continued to be strong. Notable among these was the subordinate, or, as traditionalists would say, the distinct, role of women which continued to be the norm, hence the almost total absence of references to women, as individuals – or indeed as a group – in this account. It should be added that Gentile records of the period, other than those of the Inquisition, succeed equally in suppressing most female experience. The study of the major communities, for which adequate materials exist, indicates, on the whole, a balance between group conformity and individual non-conformity in all countries. Community leaders continued to exercise a political as well as a moral and religious role in seeking to ensure some measure of safety for their charges. The intellectual, political, and social currents which threatened to upset this balance will now be examined.

Notes

1 Heinrich Graetz, *History of the Jews from the Earliest Times to the Present Day*, London, Myers, 1904, vol. iv, p. 568.
2 Maurice Kriegel, *Les Juifs à la fin du Moyen Age dans l'Europe méditerranéenne*, Paris, Hachette, 1979, p. 9.
3 M. A. Shulvass, *The Jews in the World of the Renaissance*, Leiden, Brill, 1973, pp. ix–x, 1–59, 159–214.

4 Brian Pullan, *The Jews of Europe and the Inquisition of Venice, 1550–1670*, Oxford, Blackwell, 1983, pp. 160–7.
5 Israel Adler, 'The rise of art music in the Italien ghetto', in *Jewish Medieval and Renaissance Studies*, ed Alexander Altmann, Cambridge, Mass., Harvard University Press, 1967, pp. 321–64.
6 Baron, *A Social and Religious History of the Jews*, xvi, *Poland–Lithuania, 1500–1650*, 1976, pp. 75–7; Graetz, *History*, iv, pp. 671–82.
7 Menasseh ben Israel, *The Hope of Israel*, ed Henry Méchoulan and Gérard Nahon, Oxford, Oxford University Press, 1987, pp. 1–22; Baron, op.cit., xv, pp. 33–66; Yosef Kaplan, 'The social functions of the *herem* in the Portuguese Jewish community of Amsterdam in the seventeenth century', in *Dutch Jewish History*, ed Jozeph Mishman and Tirtsah Levie, Leiden, Brill, 1984, pp. 111–55.

6

Spiritual crisis and toleration

The phrase 'spiritual crisis' has frequently been applied to the sixteenth and seventeenth centuries, and not least by Jonathan Israel. He regards the improvements which took place in the conditions of life for Jews in various parts of Europe as having been largely due to the disintegration of 'Christendom' into separate churches and sects. The Jews thus profited, both from the resulting chaos in Christian minds and from the fatigue which was induced by the many 'religious' wars of the period. The question of whether or not this 'spiritual crisis' actually took place may be approached from two directions, firstly the intellectual developments of the period and secondly the practical changes which may have taken place in the social life of Jews as a result of new policies on the part of the non-Jewish majority. The latter point will involve further consideration of the validity of the concept of 'toleration', which has already arisen in relation to the Netherlands. While it will be possible to show a gradual collapse of the intellectual edifice of late medieval Catholicism in the works of certain important learned figures in the sixteenth and seventeenth centuries, it will be necessary to go outside strictly 'intellectual' circles in order to assess the extent to which such ideas influenced other people. If they did not, or else did so to an insignificant extent, then it will scarcely be appropriate to cite the so-called 'crisis' of belief as a factor in changing the circumstances of Jews, though the whole matter might turn out differently in the case of cultural and religious developments within the Jewish communities themselves. The phrase 'spiritual crisis' is not easy to define. It is evidently associated with such phenomena as a collapse of belief in a previously accepted set of religious or general intellectual concepts, which may lead to psychological upheaval at the personal or the communal level. What is harder to trace is the transition from an individual's personal crisis to that of a whole society. In addition, a crisis may, strictly speaking, be ultimately settled in favour of a return to the person's, or the society's, original beliefs and values. Neither is it simple, even after accepting the validity of the concept of 'spiritual crisis', to place it chronologically. A good starting point will be the remark of Lucien Febvre, in his inspiring and magisterial study of Rabelais' so-called 'atheism'. 'Since the seventeenth century and the time of Descartes generations of men have made an inventory of space, analysed it and organised it. . . . This great undertaking had hardly begun in the sixteenth century.'[1] The extent to which subsequent research has demonstrated the truth of this observation will shortly become plain, but at this stage it is simply necessary to note that a considerable time-lag may be expected between the thinking of dissident and subversive thoughts by individuals, and any repercussions in public life.

Firstly, it is important to define more precisely the nature of the intellectual questionings which took place in the sixteenth and seventeenth centuries, and set them in their historical context. At the simplest level, of course, the upheavals of the sixteenth century did allow to develop, in Israel's phrase, 'proliferating assortment of sceptics, Jehovanists, deists, and other anti-Trinitarians and non-Christians of every hue'.[2] It is much easier to describe the various expressions of religious belief, or unbelief, which might be found in Europe in and after 1600 than it is to explain how they came about. However, the very diversity of these views and practices and the comparative speed with which they emerged, in relation, for example, to the many earlier centuries which had been dominated by Catholicism, together suggest that unorthodox ideas had very probably existed long before the end of the sixteenth century. When Febvre wrote in 1942, he could not of course know what valuable research would be done, to a large extent as a sequel to his pioneering efforts, on religious belief and practice in the late medieval and early

modern periods. It is still useful, however, to begin a consideration of the nature of religious belief with some of his words
on the concept most associated, in the modern mind, with
radicalism and modernity, that is, 'atheism'. In trying Rabelais
for this offence, and finding him innocent, Febvre had to stress
the different way in which the word was used in the sixteenth
century. 'If a man proclaimed that he did not think about things
exactly the way everyone else did, if he was bold in speech and
quick to criticise, people said, "He is impious. A blasphemer."
And they finished with, "An atheist!"'[3] These are important
thoughts, and of course they led Febvre to his conclusion that the
intellectual universe, at least up to the early seventeenth century,
was extremely conservative, despite the changes taking place in
institutional religion. The case is certainly a strong one, but there
is now far more information available about the religious and
general intellectual attitudes of all kinds of people. Much of this
material is to be found in the files of the Inquisition, and the
effectiveness of such documentation, when intelligently
exploited, has already been demonstrated in the case of Venice,
although the reliability of testimony to the tribunals of the Holy
Office is still very much questioned by some scholars.

The conclusions which are emerging from the study of records
from various parts of Europe – particularly from France, Italy,
and Spain – from the earliest days of the Inquisition in the
thirteenth century up to the very period under consideration
here, indicate certain deep-rooted, extensive, and persistent
phenomena of religious dissidence, involving Jews, or ex-Jews, as
well as 'cradle' Christians. The researches of R. I. Moore are
increasingly revealing a similar picture in the two preceding
centuries as well.[4] Many of the recurring manifestations of dissidence consisted, inevitably, of opposition to the institutional,
social and political power of the Catholic Church. For many
people, this took the form of anti-clericalism, an attack on the
agents of the Church with which all the population came into
daily contact. It certainly seems reasonable to argue that, in this
as in other cases, there is at least a very strong link between the
theological questioning of the nature of the priesthood by
Wycliffe and other academic thinkers, and the type of attitude
embodied in the utterance reported to have been made, in the

northern Spanish town of Soria in 1502, by a local scrivener, Gonzalo Gómez, to the effect that, 'he was amazed that, since there were such bad clergy in Soria, they could turn a little bit of material bread into the body of Our Lord'.[5] This is so despite the obvious fact that there is no evidence of any conceivable connection between a Castilian scribe and one of the recognizable heretical movements of the period, such as Lollardy or Hussitism. Blasphemy, too, was a constant method by which individuals might relieve feelings of frustration and despair at their fate, if only in their failure to win at gambling or sport. However, over and over again, the inquisitors found evidence of intellectual rejection of the doctrinal claims of Christianity. In Toulouse in the 1270s, for example, the Inquisition was looking for Cathar heretics, but it also found, in Walter Wakefield's words, people who had shown,

> disrespect for sacred things by dirty jokes, defilement of cemeteries, disparagement of the reputed holiness of saints and shrines, scepticism about the sign of the cross, quarrels with priests over burial practices, restlessness at sermons, and disparagement of conventional attitudes towards Jews and usury.

However, things sometimes went further, so that,

> these words and acts were also accompanied by more serious divergences from contemporary orthodoxy, statements often tinged with rationalism, scepticism, and revealing something of a materialistic attitude.[6]

All this appears to be what Grado Merlo called, in relation to the work of the Turin Inquisition in the 1370s and 1380s, 'the humus of religious nonconformity'. There, the main enemy, in the inquisitors' minds, was either Catharism or Waldensianism, but they also discovered individuals who rejected Christian teaching on life after death, and even the doctrine of the incarnation of Jesus. The 'universalist' strand, which gave Jews and Muslims an equal chance of salvation with Christians, also seems to have existed throughout the later Middle Ages in various countries.

Bishop Fournier, for example, in the famous interrogations in the French Pyrenean region in the early fourteenth century which brought to light the deeds and beliefs of the villagers of Montaillou, also found one Arnaud Gélis, who apparently believed, along with some followers, that

> the souls of Jews, their penance completed, go to Rest like the souls of the Christians, and it is found according to the witnesses that he says that Saint Mary, at the Judgement, will intercede for the souls of all the Jews, because they were of her race, and that all the Jews will be saved at the prayer of Saint Mary.[7]

Thus, when the Friulian miller, Domenico Scandella, alias Menocchio, told the Franciscan inquisitor and canonist Gerolamo Asteo, in 1599, that, 'I believe that each person holds his faith to be right, but we do not know which is the right one', and that 'the majesty of God has given the Holy Spirit to all, to Christians, to heretics, to Turks, and to Jews: and he considers them all dear, and they are all saved in the same manner', he was continuing a venerable tradition in ordinary people's thought about the existence of different religions in the world.[8]

At this point, however, the discussion must be widened. In his study of Menocchio's beliefs and trials, Carlo Ginzburg constantly bears in mind the question of the transmission of religious views from educated to uneducated people. This is a vital, and highly controversial, matter. For many scholars currently engaged in work on religious belief and practice in the medieval and early modern periods, it is no longer possible to accept without question views such as those recently expressed by Bruce Lenman, to the effect that, 'a great deal of popular piety in the medieval, and indeed in the early modern period was clearly syncretist in nature'. Condoned by the Church, 'It combined attitudes to pagan magic-making with Christian forms.'[9] As Jim Obelkevich rightly warns, the religion of the people 'is religion. To treat it as ignorance, superstition, debasement, as compensation, or mystification, is to misconceive it.'[10] The word 'superstition' needs particularly to be watched. It is, as William Monter has noted, 'a remarkably durable and highly flexible pejorative term'. Having been used by sophisticated Romans to describe the religion of the less educated,

> it was adapted by the Christians to ridicule the old Roman state religion, and by the medieval Church to condemn the 'barbarous' folk beliefs of northern Europeans. At the Reformation, Protestants turned the word against a great many Catholic practices unknown to Scripture of which they disapproved.[11]

The problem, less clearly alluded to by Monter, is that more recent scholars, whether religious believers or not, have tended, when discussing the religious lives of others, to adopt one or other of the definitions of superstition which were devised in earlier periods by one group of believers or another. Commonly, though, the reader is not made aware in the text of the assumptions and choices which have been made by the author. It must be clear that, in fact, one person's 'religion' can very easily be another's 'superstition', in any period of history and in any school of historical study. The term, in other words, is as elusive and chameleon-like as the description 'atheist', and at this stage it may be best to return, duly warned, to the question of the relationship, if any, between educated and uneducated religious dissidence, and thus attempt to characterize the intellectual climate of the sixteenth and seventeenth centuries.

In order to do this, it is useful to return to the Friulian miller. Menocchio had one important characteristic which distinguished him from most of his contemporaries and medieval predecessors. He was literate. This meant that his knowledge of the world was gained, not only from his senses and the spoken word, but also from that hallmark of the Renaissance, the printed page. For Ginzburg, the addition of reading-matter to the old sources of information was devastating. 'It was not the book as such, but the encounter between the printed page and oral culture that formed an explosive mixture in Menocchio's head.'[12] However, it is perhaps even more interesting for the present purpose that Ginzburg attempts to link the miller's views on religious toleration with those of an intellectual from France, a pupil and colleague of Calvin, Sebastian Castellio. Without any evidence of a

direct link of the kind beloved of those who regard the
uneducated as an inert mass awaiting instruction from the
learned, whether through personal contact or reading, it seems
that Scandella and Castellio arrived at the same all-embracing
definition of religious toleration. The issue which led Castellio to
oppose his master and publish, in 1554, under the pseudonym
Martin Bellius, a book entitled *On Heretics, and Whether they
should be Persecuted*, was the burning in Geneva, in the
previous year, of the Spaniard Michael Servetus, for his rejection
of the doctrine of the Trinity, which Catholics and Protestants
shared. Castellio, in this work, put Scripture firmly above
theological doctrine, and attempted to show that the Bible did
not allow for the execution of heretics. Indeed it only recognized
the concept of 'heretic' in one place, Paul's letter to Titus, and
even there it appeared that the punishment envisaged by the
apostle for false belief was excommunication not death, and that
only after the third offence. Already, in 1551, Castellio had
expressed doubts about current practice in the repression of
heresy, from which the Anabaptists and various anti-Trinitarian
groups were particularly suffering. He stated that religious
'truths' were not self-evident to everyone. 'We ought certainly,
however much we may think we know everything, we ought, I
say, to fear lest in crucifying thieves justly we crucify also Christ
unjustly.' This honest uncertainty about religious dogma led the
Frenchman to advocate, in his 1554 preface, that the concept of a
'heretic' should be abandoned altogether. With disturbing
clarity and perceptiveness, he noted that a 'heretic' was simply a
person with whom one disagreed about religion, and 'there is
practically no sect which does not hold all others for heretics'. For
him, it was quite wrong that doctrinal error or disagreement
should be far more seriously regarded than moral offences, such
as murder or adultery. He also cited supporters among his contemporaries. Perhaps not surprisingly, his main ally was the Ana-
baptist leader Sebastian Franck, a Catholic priest who had
become a Lutheran in 1527, but quickly moved towards a more
libertarian faith. His withdrawal from the main dogmatic battles
between Catholics and Protestants was based on his simple view
of the true nature of religion. For him, 'the cross alone is the
Christian's theology', and this understanding led him to adopt

openness towards the dogmas of all faiths. He stated, 'We know in part. Socrates was right, that we know only that we do not know. We may be heretics quite as much as our opponents.' With dogma cleared away, religious freedom would truly come about at last. 'Where the spirit of God is, there is freedom – no constraint, tyranny, partisanship or compulsion.' Instead, and Castellio quoted these words in full:

> I have my brothers among the Turks, Papists, Jews and all peoples. Not that they are Turks, Jews, Papists and Sectaries or will remain so; in the evening they will be called into the vineyard and given the same wage as we.

In his work, Castellio added, 'The better a man knows the truth, the less is he inclined to condemn.'[13] Henry Kamen points out that Castellio had little direct influence on his contemporaries, although the later anti-Trinitarians, for example in Poland, did develop further his doctrine of toleration as a reaction to their own sufferings. However, it is important at this stage to consider whether the views of Franck and Castellio had any parallel in learned circles, as they clearly did among the uneducated.

Here, the crucial figure is Erasmus, who, in his own mind, had already pared away much of the dogmatic baggage of late medieval Catholicism. The radical nature of his views was long ago demonstrated by Febvre. The sacraments, on which much of the religious life of late medieval Catholics depended, were shown up in an entirely new light, in which their efficacy no longer depended on correctness of form and administration, but on the personal quality of both administrator and recipient. Thus, in his *Enchiridion* or *Guide for the Christian Soldier*, he warned, 'You are baptized, but do not therefore think you are a Christian.' A pagan, with right intention, is more a Christian than someone who is baptized but lacks the desire to lead a Christian life. Likewise, for the Dutch humanist, intention became the vital feature of the main sacrament of the Church, the mass, or communion. Both Febvre and later scholars, such as Bossy, have stressed the difference between late medieval and early modern Eucharistic practice on the one hand and modern Catholic ideas on the other. Communion was rarely taken, even by the most devout, so that personal devotion to the sacrament did not, in the sixteenth century, take the form it was to acquire in later centuries.[14] In this sense, Erasmus was not outstandingly radical. His fundamental understanding of the Christian faith was extremely simple. He once said it was 'nothing else but true and perfect friendship'. In stressing, therefore, the sociable aspects of the mass, its sealing of the bond between Christ, 'our prince', and his friends the disciples, Erasmus appeared to be continuing the medieval tradition which saw the sacrament as a socially cohesive act, particularly in the rituals of the 'peace' and the passing round of the consecrated bread of fellowship, which allowed those other than the presiding clergy to participate physically in the sacred meal. In reality though, the mystical content of the mass had been removed by the humanist's interpretation, and both Zwingli and the group known as the Sacramentarians took the point and developed it into a systematic dogma, of the very type which its originator abhorred. For Erasmus, then, everything depended on the communicant's attitude, as Paul had indeed warned in the New Testament itself. However, the ancient friendship rites, rather than the Jewish Passover meal, or *seder*, became for him the origin of the mass, and thus another link between Christianity and Judaism was severed. Febvre argues that Erasmus's dualism was not only applied in order to support the Christian reading of the Old Testament as a 'spiritual' book, but also extended to the New, in such a way as to remove all personal content from the life of Christ, as recounted there, and hence from devotion to the suffering Jesus and the following of the Way of the Cross, which played such an important part in the religious life of the period. Thus the Dutchman's genuinely simple, 'evangelical', faith, in effect though not in intention removed much of the human and affective from Christianity. In Febvre's words, Jesus's death and passion were,

> so many allegories to be interpreted by the elect; the mob, however, bound to the concrete, did not perceive their deep significance. Christ was a precept, a moral doctrine, nothing else but the virtues he preached – charity, simplicity, patience, purity.[15]

All this seems to imply a large gap between the learned and the unlearned, but even in Erasmus's work there are direct links with the more general scepticism, though not the materialism, which has already been noted in some members of the population at large. The issue over which the humanist of Rotterdam seems to have shared some common ground with humbler predecessors and contemporaries was the nature of the afterlife. He stated plainly that, 'the infernal flames were only a figure of speech of the Gospel. To follow the path of Christ was to prepare one's entrance into a *felicitas* (happiness) whose nature he did not tell us about: his Paradise lacked imagination.'[16] Thus the fires of Hell, suffered by the evil, were in fact a mental phenomenon. They represented the gnawing of the conscience of a person who had knowingly offended against the moral code which Jesus taught.

All this needs to be considered in a wider context. If Erasmus's followers tried to keep his ideas alive, 'simple as they were, lacking in dogmatism [except towards Judaism!] and expressed in sensitive language by a mind that professed a horror of grand statements, the cultivation of irony, respect for decorum',[17] how many others thought in the same way, and was the edifice of Christian belief really crumbling? By 1550, Calvin had certainly come to think that it was. He blamed individuals, such as the great French writer, François Rabelais, the minor French humanist, Bernardine des Périers, and the Portuguese Antonio de Gouvea. The aim of these men, he asserted, was to 'abolish all reverence for God'. They stated openly, he claimed, that 'all religions have been formed in the brains of men; that we think there is a God because we like to believe it; that hope of life eternal is something to amuse idiots with; that everything said about Hell is done to frighten little children'.[18] How strongly Calvin's words resemble those supposedly said in the northern Spanish village of Peroniel del Campo (Soria), one day in 1494, by Diego de Barrionuevo, a villager, 'I swear to God that this Hell and Paradise is nothing more than a way of frightening us, like people saying to children, "Avati coco!" ["The bogeyman will get you!"].'[19] At times, the barrier between 'learned' and 'unlearned' religious thought is so permeable as to be effectively non-existent. It is hardly likely that Diego had read Erasmus, but the Soria inquisitors were no more keen than Calvin on such views, 'modern' as they sound.

There were also, increasingly in the sixteenth century, learned men who shared Menocchio and Franck's views on religious 'universalism'. One of them was the French humanist, Guillaume Postel. In his massive Latin work, *A Book to Reconcile the Koran, or Law of Mohammed, and that of the Evangelists*, published in 1543, Postel set out a blueprint for achieving the moral unity of the universe, by persuading not only divided Christians, Jews, and Muslims, but also the newly discovered peoples of America, Africa, and the East, to join a reformed, ecumenical 'church' which would broaden the Catholic faith of his own day so that it came to be identical with what he regarded as the innate 'natural' religion of all people. This would consist of an undogmatic desire to pour out one's gratitude to God the creator for all his works, and to seek to possess God for all eternity. The notions of cursing or excommunicating other believers, and condemning them for 'heresy', would thus disappear from the world. Postel seems to have been somewhat unstable in his personal life. His celebrations of the Catholic mass were said by a contemporary, Florimond de Raiemond to be remarkable spiritual experiences, in which they might see, 'his long white beard, his majestic air, his eyes darting flames like carbuncles, and the smoke rising from his hoary head at the moment of consecration . . . "so intently did he concentrate on this mystery"'.[20] However, Postel remained firmly in a Catholic Christian context despite his extreme eccentricity and his clear sense not only that there were large parts of the world, some of them known to him as an orientalist, in which Christianity existed scarcely if at all, but also that Christendom itself was now crumbling as a result of internal disputes. His 'universalism' was certainly not the result of doubt or scepticism, but rather an afterglow of the earlier, medieval ideas of a worldwide 'Christendom', such as had lain behind the legend of the Christian emperor, Prester John, in Africa. The Christianity of Postel, weird and idiosyncratic as it was, found itself completely surpassed in radicality by the religious thought of the political philosopher, Jean Bodin. This has recently been reinterpreted by Paul Rose, and the results are of great importance to the consideration of the relationship between Christianity and Judaism which developed at the intellectual level in the latter part of the sixteenth century. Rose argues that Bodin actually abandoned the medieval Christian intellectual edifice, which other early modern thinkers largely maintained, and replaced it with an entirely Jewish system of religion, derived from the Ancient Philo of Alexandria and the medieval Maimonides. Rose finds the evidence for this particularly in Bodin's *Paradox*, not published in Latin until 1596, and in French until 1598 when the French religious wars were coming to an end, and even more in his dialogue between seven religious speakers, the *Heptaplomeres*, which was completed in Bodin's last years, between 1588 and his death of the plague in 1596.[21]

The argument runs as follows. To begin with it has to be noted that Bodin's religious development underlay his written views on politics, including the place of the Jews in European society. An important influence on his attitude to religion was his training in the Carmelite house in Paris in the mid- and late 1540s. The Carmelite order, in existence since the early thirteenth century, had the prophet Elijah as its spiritual founder, and practised a secluded or eremitical life involving meditation on God, which was intended to lead a close communion with Him, and hence to spiritual illumination for the disciple. The importance of the relatively brief spell which Bodin spent with the order was not only that it seems to have taught him the meditative techniques and aims which he was to retain for the rest of his life, but also that it led him to stress the gift of prophecy, which the Carmelites respected highly because of the activity of their Jewish father. Elijah had, in any case, a prominent place in the Christian beliefs concerning the Last Days. Following on from apocalyptic passages in both Old and New Testaments, Christians generally believed that the second coming of Jesus would be heralded by the reappearance of Elijah, and such views became entangled, in Spain around the year 1500, with *conversos'* desire to be delivered from the persecution of the Inquisition. In the process, individuals from the New Christian communities, particularly in New Castile and Andalusia, such as Inés in Herrera del Duque and Bachelor Alonso de Membreque in Córdoba, themselves took up the prophetic ministry, foretelling the coming of Elijah and the Messiah, and the deliverance of the *conversos*.[22]

Bodin's activity, on the other hand, was intellectual rather than practical. He seems, in the midst of his career, to have rejected the central theological tenets of Christianity, that is to say, the reality of the 'original sin' of every member of human-kind, and the need of a 'saviour' to make atonement to God for that sin and 'redeem' all those who accepted the 'salvation' thus offered. These terms, from the technical language of theology, are still often taken for granted. It is remarkable therefore that Bodin should have rejected so much of the Christian heritage into which he was born, and accepted an entirely different ex-planation of the world and its problems. Bodin did not become an 'atheist', in the sense of abandoning his belief in the one God, creator of the world and everything in it. He was a mono-theist, but he differed from all strands of Christianity in his own day, even from those which 'judaized', by adhering in some way to Jewish ritual observances. He was not at all interested in the ritual practice of Judaism, which so much dominated the rabbin-ical discipline and community life of contemporary Jews. Instead, he adopted a thought-form which was fairly alien to most medieval and early modern Jews, that is, a 'theological' Judaism. It was no accident that he went to the two earlier figures, Philo and Maimonides, who had attempted to understand and communicate their Judaism in ways which were comprehensible to the non-Jewish intellectuals of their own day. In other words, they adopted the customary philosophical terminology of the ancient and medieval worlds, which was derived in large part from Greek thinkers, such as Plato and Aris-totle, and the Stoics. Bodin, in that sense, as the inheritor of the work of the Jewish philosophers, was not moving away from the intellectual habits of learned Christians of his own day, or their medieval predecessors. What made him innovative among Christians was his adoption of the Jewish understanding of human nature and the problem of evil, instead of the Christian one – which gave the central role to Jesus in the salvation of an intrinsically sinful human race. Like the Jews, Bodin continued to recognize that all human beings are sinful, but he now saw this, not as the inevitable result of Adam's eating the forbidden fruit in the garden of Eden, but rather of wrong choices made by the free will of individual human beings. Salvation thus came about through a conscious decision to lead a righteous life, rather than the vicarious redemption offered by Jesus, the son of God.

In the process, the whole Christian doctrine of the atonement, and the teaching surrounding the birth, ministry, passion, death, and resurrection of Jesus was undermined, and consigned to irrelevance. Bodin's thought was, except in the *Hepta-plomeres* artfully concealed behind what appeared to be conventional Christian discourse. It did not have much direct influence, in its own day or afterwards, but it is perhaps interesting to conclude this consideration of one of the first 'intellectuals' to escape altogether from the traditional Christian framework of thought with a comparative example of humbler Christians who also found the doctrine of the incarnation, as well as the rest of Christology, implausible and even offensive. In the mid-1490s, for instance, a Spanish broker said in Soria, when observing the devotions in the town which commemorated the sufferings of Jesus, 'What man living is there who would believe that God put Himself under such temptation? and that he [Jesus] was son of God? What father would there be who would push his son into a thing like this?' On Easter Sunday in the same year, a woman in Soria was supposed to have gone further and said, 'May I be cursed by God if I can believe that it happened like that, rather that someone got it all up to do harm to the Jews.'[23]

The point to be made about the religious dissent of Spaniards in the late fifteenth and early sixteenth centuries is that it seems in many cases to have originated from the discontent of converts with their new religion. In Spain and Portugal, there were to be bouts of arrests, interrogations, and punishment of converts and their descendants until at least as late as 1700. It is important, though, to look at the spiritual trends among unbaptized Jews throughout Europe after 1492, and if possible relate them to the intellectual activity then going on in Christian circles. If this is done, it will for example be possible to assess the reality of fears concerning 'judaizing' among Christians, which became, and continued to be, prominent throughout the sixteenth century. Before examining the three main trends in specifically Jewish spirituality in this period, that is to say, Kabbalah, messianism, and rationalism, it is important to note that, in considering intellectual currents in both religions, no assumption should be made that there was a 'linear' development from belief to unbelief, from faith to scepticism, from irrationality to rationality, or even from 'superstition' to 'religion'. The revival of a wish to identify with Judaism among lifelong Christians of Jewish descent from the Iberian Peninsula, who passed through or lived in Venice and Amsterdam, for example, illustrates a kind of 'throwback' which has been found in other circumstances and periods up to the present day. Equally, there might be reactions against rationalistic and sceptical tendencies, and a return to orthodoxy, which constituted a response to suffering and upheaval.

Kabbalism

There is good reason to suppose that such was the case with Judaism, during and after the expulsion of Jews from Spain and other parts of western Europe. Much of the spiritual life of Jewish communities in both eastern and western Europe arose from the revival of Kabbalistic studies originating in the land of Israel itself. Central to this was the Galilean town of Safed, where refugees from Spain and Portugal, and to a lesser extent from Italy and Germany, gathered during the sixteenth century to study the Law in the tradition (that being the very meaning of the word 'Kabbalah') which had originated in thirteenth-century France. Israel rightly regards this movement as 'the most powerful factor shaping early modern Jewish culture'. The main figures were Moses Cordovero, a Spanish Jew, and Isaac Luria, an Ashkenazi, who moved to Safed in his later life. Although his sayings were only published in written form by his disciples, Luria was perhaps the most prominent thinker in the Kabbalistic revival. His ideas quickly spread to other areas of Jewish settlement, and in particular the Balkans and Italy. What he and his followers offered to Jews was a revised notion of the role of the Messiah. Divine intervention, it was alleged, in order to end evil in the world and finish the sufferings of the Jews (an outcome which all Orthodox believed to be inevitable in due course), would only happen when events had reached a certain point, made possible only by Jews co-operating sufficiently with God by means of their own positive actions. Thus it was not the Messiah's responsibility to bring about the redemption of the world, but rather that of the whole Jewish people, who would achieve mystical communion with God by means of Orthodox worship, and righteous acts in fulfilment of the commandments of the Law. Luria's vision of human co-operation with God in the overcoming of evil gave every individual the chance to help achieve his or her messianic dream. The Kabbalists of Galilee in the late sixteenth century took part in midnight devotions, supplementing Orthodox tradition, in which they sought, by their prayer and action, to produce not only renewed unity among humankind, but also reconciliation within the Godhead, between the feminine principle of *Shekinah* and the other divine emanations. If the ex-Christian Bodin found intellectual satisfaction in the notion of human free will, then the Kabbalah of Safed afforded Orthodox Jews a chance to participate directly in the divine purpose, and thus regain, perhaps, the self-respect which their straitened social and economic circumstances might threaten to remove from them.[24]

Messianism

The messianic movement, in the traditional style, was by no means dead in early modern Jewry. Stephen Sharot has identi-fied, from the sociologist's point of view, a distinction between Sephardic and Ashkenazi Jewry in their reaction to suffering in this period. He regards the difference as an important part of the explanation of the increased belief of the Sephardim in the imminent arrival of the Messiah to deliver them from their trials at Christian and, in North Africa, Muslim hands, in contrast to the more passive resignation which centuries of oppression and marginalization had induced among the Ashkenazim.[25] Certainly, Abravanel and others attempted to interpret the expulsion from Spain as a precursor of the arrival of the Messianic age, but, just as the Kabbalistic revival in Galilee transcended the historic and cultural divisions between the two main branches of Judaism, so the remarkable messianic movement of Sabbatai Sevi in the second half of the seventeenth century overcame all kinds of social and political barriers, and swept nearly all sectors of European Jewry. As its main student, Gershom Scholem, has pointed out, the Sabbatean movement disregarded any 'social' or 'class' theory of religion, and revealed, in the starkest manner, the limits on the growth of 'rationalism' in seventeenth-century

Europe. The response of some of the richest Jews of Amsterdam was the same as that of their poorest co-religionaries in the Balkans and elsewhere, for a period of months after the news of his prophecies, visions and miracles spread to Europe; the Jew from Smyrna, having overcome all opposition to his mystical claims, in the Near East, and, with the help and encouragement of the more organized and energetic Nathan of Gaza, proclaimed himself Messiah in May 1665. Despite much Christian mockery, which is more likely to have arisen from traditional anti-Judaism than from rationalism, most Jews seem to have regarded Sabbatai's claims as genuine, and as an opportunity for them to be freed from the limitations and restrictions of their current life. The conversion of the so-called Messiah to Islam, which followed his summons to Constantinople by the Sultan in September 1666, apparently brought the messianic hope to an abrupt and humiliating end. Nevertheless, Nathan of Gaza continued to spread the word, even after the Messiah's death in 1676, interpreting his sufferings and conversion as messianic signs in themselves, and his death as unreal. By 1685 there was a community in Salonika known as the Donmeh, which, while publicly Islamic, was secretly Jewish, and survived until 1925. It is of course hard, if not impossible, to estimate the effect of a movement which touched Jewish morale and self-perception, rather than practical living conditions. However, Sabbatai's meteoric rise and fall must serve to indicate the deep yearning which existed, in all parts of Jewish society, in Europe and the Near East, for deliverance from alien rule and restoration to a successful independence, if possible in the land of Israel itself. In this respect at least, the *conversos* of Spain shared fully in the aspirations of their brothers and sisters who continued in the old religion. The response to Sabbatai Sevi raises fundamental questions about the gains which Jews perceived themselves to have made in European society in this period, whatever later historians may suppose.[26]

Rationalism

The success of Kabbalism and messianism among the Jews of Europe in the sixteenth and seventeenth centuries must also cause doubts concerning one other development traditionally regarded as significant – the Jewish contribution to the growth of a rationalistic and sceptical frame of mind among certain educated sections of society. It has already been indicated that, in Christian terms, if there is indeed such a phenomenon in this period, it involves not so much the discovery of new ideas and approaches, for example to religion, but rather the conversion of certain long-standing opinions among ordinary people into intellectually respectable options. The fact that Jews are commonly connected with this aspect of European intellectual history is mainly due to the work of Baruch Spinoza, who lived in the Netherlands as an almost exact contemporary of Sabbati Sevi. They represented extremes of rationalism and faith which, in a sense, outdid those of the Christian diversity of the period. Spinoza was a Sephardi, born into the relative intellectual freedom of seventeenth-century Amsterdam. He began with Orthodox Talmudic studies, then was attracted by the work of the rationalistic Frenchman, René Descartes and his followers, and entered from that side the controversies which were already raging in the Sephardic community over such questions as whether heretics and apostates would in fact suffer eternal punishment, as traditional Judaism and Christianity both claimed. Earlier in the century the rabbis had still been strong enough to have Uriel da Costa whipped for heresy, but in the 1650s a small group, led at first by Dr Juan de Prado, began to take the new sceptical ideas further. Prado was a Spanish physician, who had lived in France for a while as a New Christian, but who, soon after returning to Judaism in Amsterdam in 1655, was condemned with Spinoza for 'unspeakable blasphemies' and put under rabbinical ban. Prado and Spinoza both eventually left Judaism, the latter joining an obscure group of radical Dutch Protestants, and living on pensions from Christian patrons and an income from grinding lenses. In 1663 he published a work in Latin and Dutch on Descartes' philosophy, but his most famous and significant work is his *Tractatus Theologico-Politicus* of 1670, which presented a somewhat diluted version of his views on religion and politics. Monter has described the *Tractatus* as 'an apologia for the bland religious toleration pursued by De Witt's republican administration'.[27] He perhaps underestimates the power of Spinoza's advocacy of freedom of religion and speech, although he admits that the Jew went further than John Locke and as far as the French Enlightenment figure, Pierre Bayle. Clearly strongly influenced by the passions aroused as a result of the current religious disputes in the Netherlands, in which Jews were not directly involved, he concluded that,

> the safest way for a state is to lay down the rule that religion is comprised solely in the exercise of charity and justice, and that the rights of rulers in sacred, no less than in secular matters, should merely have to do with actions, but that every man should think what he likes and say what he thinks.

In a devastating critique of the religious controversies of his own day, and the way in which religious authorities and governments of all persuasions claimed to be certain of the truth and tried to enforce adherence to it, Spinoza wrote, 'that schisms do not originate in a love of truth, which is a source of courtesy and gentleness, but rather in an inordinate desire for supremacy', thus, 'the real disturbers of the peace are those who, in a free state, seek to curtail the liberty of judgement which they are unable to tyrannise over'.[28]

Such views obviously appealed to individuals, who had an interest, in some cases professional, in the free expression and traffic of ideas. However, in practical terms, they clearly reflected the peculiar political conditions of the Netherlands after 1650. None the less, Spinoza had appeal, and his followers in France, England, and Germany after 1670 were commonly known as Spinozans, as indeed were all those in Europe who appeared to share his philosophical views. In political terms his time had not of course arrived, and indeed his robust and complete defence of freedom of thought has rarely, if ever, been adequately applied since. The religious part of the work, however, contains material so radical that its implications cause turmoil in some cases even today. Spinoza said little about the New Testament, as he was mainly addressing his own people. He did, however, point to the contrast which may be made between Paul's view that salvation might be obtained by faith, or 'faith alone' as Luther said, and James's statement of the necessity for faith to be shown forth in practical works, if a person was to lead a good Christian life.

Interestingly, the Dutch Sephardi saw the New Testament very much as a Jewish book, saying that the Apostles were not prophets, but teachers who taught the essential religion of Judaism, which was, as in Deuteronomy, belief in, and obedience to, the one God, and the love of one's neighbour as much as oneself. In the *Tractatus*, however, he followed in some respects the tradition of 'rational' objection to Christianity which had so often been expressed in medieval polemic and disputation. Like so many rabbis of the past, including Nachmanides in thirteenth-century Spain, he found the Christological and Trinitarian teaching of Christianity incomprehensible. Thus, while he was happy to accept that God spoke through Jesus, as he had through Moses, he added, 'I must at this juncture declare that those doctrines which certain churches put forward concerning Christ, I neither affirm or deny, for I freely confess that I do not understand them.' However, Christianity was only an incidental target for Spinoza. His main aim was to demolish the irrational edifice, as he saw it, of traditional Judaism. Thus he asserted that 'the power of prophecy implies not a peculiarly perfect mind, but a peculiarly vivid imagination', and that, 'We may . . . be absolutely certain that every event which is truly described in Scripture necessarily happened, like everything else, according to natural laws.'[29] For him, the ritual precepts of the Mosaic Law had no valid application outside Israel itself, and therefore the Jews of the Diaspora should not cling to them, but simply pursue, along with the Gentiles, an understanding of the Divine which was within the compass of an entirely human understanding and capacity, and which corresponded to the divinely ordained natural laws of the universe.

Notes

1 Lucien Febvre, *The Problem of Unbelief in the Sixteenth Century. The Religion of Rabelais*, Cambridge, Mass., and London, Harvard University Press, 1982, p. 100.
2 Jonathan Israel, *European Jewry in the Age of Mercantilism, 1550–1750*, Oxford, Clarendon Press, 1985, p. 258.
3 Febvre, *Unbelief*, p. 131.
4 See, for example, R. I. Moore, *The Origins of European Dissent*, rev. edn, Oxford, Blackwell, 1985.

5 Carlos Carrete Parrondo, ed., *El Tribunal de la Inquisición en el Obispado de Soria (1486–1502), Fontes Iudaeorum Regni Castellae*, ii, Salamanca, Pontifical University of Salamanca and University of Granada, 1985, no. 135 p. 72.

6 Walter L. Wakefield, 'Some unorthodox popular ideas of the thirteenth century', *Medievalia et Humanistica*, iv (1973), 29.

7 Jean Duvernoy, *Le registre d'Inquisition de Jacques Fournier*, Paris, Mouton, 1978, i, 166–7.

8 Carlo Ginzburg, *The Cheese and the Worms. The Cosmos of a Sixteenth-century Miller*, London, Routledge & Kegan Paul, 1980, p. 51.

9 Bruce Lenman, 'The limits of godly discipline in the early modern period with particular reference to England and Scotland', in *Religion and Society in Early Modern Europe, 1500–1800*, ed Kaspar von Greyerz, London, George Allen & Unwin and German Historical Institute, 1984, p. 126.

10 Jim Obelkevich, *Religion and the People, 800–1700*, Chapel Hill, North Carolina University Press, 1979, p. 7.

11 William Monter, *Ritual, Myth and Magic in Early Modern Europe*, Brighton, Harvester, 1983, p. 114.

12 Ginzburg, *Cheese*, p. 51.

13 Henry Kamen, *The Rise of Toleration*, London, Weidenfeld & Nicolson, 1967, pp. 77–8.

14 Febvre, *Unbelief*, pp. 159–60; John Bossy, *Christianity in the West, 1400–1700*, Oxford, Clarendon Press, 1985, pp. 66–72.

15 Febvre, *Unbelief*, pp. 321–6.

16 ibid., p. 320.

17 ibid., p. 333.

18 ibid., p. 130.

19 Carrete, *El Tribunal*, p. 125; J. H. Edwards, 'Religious faith and doubt in late medieval Spain: Soria, c. 1450–1500', *Past and Present*, forthcoming.

20 Febvre, *Unbelief*, p. 112.

21 Paul Lawrence Rose, *Bodin and the Great God of Nature. The Moral and Religious Universe of a Judaizer*, Geneva, Droz, 1980.

22 For these episodes, see John Edwards, 'Elijah and the Inquisition: messianic prophecy among *conversos* in Spain, c. 1500', *Nottingham Medieval Studies*, xxviii (1984), pp. 79–94.

23 Carrete, *El Tribunal*, pp. 80, 143.

24 Israel, *European Jewry*, pp. 78–80.

25 Stephen Sharot, 'Jewish millenarianism: a comparison of medieval communities', *Comparative Studies in Society and History*, xxii (1980), pp. 394–415.

26 Gershom Scholem, *Sabbatai Sevi, the Mystical Messiah (1626–1676)*, Princeton, Princeton University Press, 1973.

27 Monter, *Ritual*, p. 149.

28 Benedict (Baruch) de Spinoza, *A Theological-political Treatise*, trans. R. H. M. Elwes, New York, Dover, 1951, pp. 265, 264.

29 Spinoza, *Treatise*, pp. 19, 92.

7
Jews and Christians on the eve
of the Enlightenment

In 1711 a work entitled *Entdecktes Judenthum* ('Judaism
exposed') appeared in Berlin but with a false title-page showing
Königsberg as its place of publication. Its author, Johann
Andreas Eisenmenger, professor of Hebrew at Heidelberg, had
died seven years previously, after a long controversy involving the
Emperor Leopold, the leading 'Court Jew' of the period, Samson
Wertheimer, and the city authorities of Frankfurt. In a sense,
Eisenmenger's book, appearing on the eve of the rationalistic
movement known as the Enlightenment, was the culmination of
medieval anti-Judaism in its 'learned' form. It repeated all the
traditional accusations of the ritual murder of Christian children,
the poisoning of wells by Jews, particularly during the period of
the Black Death, and the evil, blasphemous, and anti-Christian
character of the Talmud. However, while it clearly shows the
continued power, even after the upheavals of the previous two
centuries, of old Christian ideas about Jews and Judaism which
were shared by learned and unlearned, the context of the writing
of Eisenmenger's work illustrates the advances which some Jews
had indeed made by the late seventeenth century in their social
and economic conditions. The professor was provoked to start
what turned into a 2,000-page work by a visit to Amsterdam in
1680–1, during which he was appalled to see the freedom in
which Jews lived, the splendour of their new places of worship,
and their ability publicly to denounce Christianity. In this respect, as well as in its actual content, the *Entdecktes Judenthum*

is an appropriate means of bringing together the intellectual activities which were considered in the previous chapter and the practical conditions in which the Jews of Europe were living, as the eighteenth century began.

It is appropriate to begin an examination of the state of the main Jewish communities with the Netherlands, where some of the greatest gains in social, economic, and religious terms had been made, especially after 1650. It was the arrival of refugees, firstly Sephardim from Spain and the failed Dutch colony in Brazil, and secondly Ashkenazim from Germany and Poland, which brought the question of Jewish settlement and civil rights towards the top of the agenda, not only in Amsterdam and Rotterdam, where a freer Jewish life had already been achieved, but also in smaller Dutch towns which had previously kept Jews out. As Israel has clearly shown, it was the economic activity of Sephardim in the West Indies which allowed greater Jewish self-assertiveness in Holland itself. From the 1660s onwards, the Amsterdam Jewish community became part of a trading triangle with the Caribbean, especially Curaçao, and Surinam in the north-east of South America. Amsterdam Jewry maintained considerable influence over the 4,000 or so Sephardim who lived in the West Indies, and the Dutch West India Company played an important part in helping Jewish economic influence to expand in this way. In 1653 the local authorities in the Spanish Netherlands, under Archduke Leopold, even tried to have openly practising Jews readmitted, and although the Spanish government and the papacy put a stop to the scheme some New Christians, led by Lopo Ramires, were allowed to move south to Antwerp. The economic activities of Dutch Jews inevitably brought them into conflict with local Christian guilds, as in Amsterdam, where after 1660 the Sephardic colonial trade was the basis of Jewish prosperity, for example in the chocolate trade. In general, it is clear that the relative religious freedom from which Dutch Jews benefited, was paralleled by economic opportunity, although, as will be seen in the case of England, these two interests did not necessarily coincide.

In France, the Jewish profile continued to be low throughout the period up to 1700, though after 1598 the public pretence of Christian conformity became less and less necessary in south-western towns such as Bayonne and Bordeaux, and communities of openly practising Jews survived in papal territory in Provence, at Carpentras for example, where Counter-Reformation policies achieved only a limited effect. The social role of these communities was mainly in trade and finance, whereas in Italy, as ever, the picture was more varied. In the late seventeenth century there were about 12,000 Jews in Rome, Venice, Livorno, Mantua, and Ferrara, with growth of population in Livorno, and also in Modena, Casale, and the area around Trieste. Thus, by 1700, the Jewish population of Italy was probably about 30,000, compared with the contemporary Jewish writer, Simone Luzzatto's estimate of 25,000 in 1637. The political structure of Italy meant that the fate of Jews always depended on their relations with individual rulers, who could quickly expand or contract a community. In economic and social terms, trade and financial services predominated in the occupational structure of Jewry, here as elsewhere. The Italian–Balkan trade route continued to be a source of employment and favours from rulers. There was also, of course, a lower group of citizens in most if not all Jewish communities, which included pedlars, hawkers, second-hand clothers-sellers, and other petty traders, craftsmen, and artisans, and the inevitable unemployed or destitute. In Venice, Jews were largely excluded from shopkeeping, though they were able to deal in tobacco and old clothes. However, they had a large role in importing the city's grain, wine, and olive oil, and also in their distribution through the towns of Venice's Italian mainland possessions. However, it was not only in the papal states that the medieval pursuits of pawnbroking and loan-making remained mainstays of Italian Jewish life.[1] The tendency was, though, for the economic importance of Italian Jewry to increase in the later seventeenth century, as did the centralizing of the government of the various communities, beginning with the new laws for Jewish internal self-government set out in Rome in 1524, to solve disputes between the various 'nations' – Italian, German, Portuguese, and Levantine. Jews in Italy succeeded in becoming involved in some of the newer trades, such as sugar-refining, tobacco-processing, and coral-polishing.

In the Empire, on the other hand, Prague provided the best opportunities for Jews, thanks to the freedom granted to them by the emperors to manufacture goods for Jewish customers, and even, in some cases, for Gentiles too. Jewish guilds were formed, to make clothes for example, and work with furs, precious metals, and leather. In Germany itself and Austria, however, where community organization, especially on a national scale, was weak, Jews were caught in an awkward economic zone. They found themselves isolated between the effects of the colonial trade which brought prosperity to Dutch communities, and Bohemia, Poland, and Lithuania, where Jews had greater freedom, with Imperial and noble support respectively, to establish their own economic structures. The result was an almost complete confinement to the provision of financial services, and the limited artisan and shopkeeping activities required to supply internal community needs. It was in Poland–Lithuania that the most comprehensive national community structure was developed, between 1550 and 1580, as a result of the peculiar political and economic circumstances of the dual Commonwealth which allowed this relative freedom to Jews. In demographic terms, western European Jewry was beginning to be re-established in the seventeenth-century, after the disasters of the fifteenth and early sixteenth centuries. If there were in 1700, as Israel calculates, about half a million Jews in Europe, including Ottoman territory, about 350,000 of them probably lived in the dual Commonwealth, a figure about ten times that of the Crown of Bohemia. Dutch Jewry, on the other hand, with about 18,000, was relatively small in numbers, although very important in economic terms.

It remains to be considered, whether the breakdown of consensus among Christian intellectuals, together with the large-scale incidence of 'religious' wars in the sixteenth and seventeenth centuries, had, as Israel asserts, a significant part to play in securing greater freedom of worship and conscience, as well as economic opportunities, for Jews. The picture which emerges from the material considered so far suggests that direct links of this kind are hard to find. Pragmatic, economic interests still generally predominated in decision-making on the fate of Jewish communities in various parts of Europe. The two cases which merit closer examination are Bohemia and England. It was noted earlier that religious toleration in the sixteenth-century Crown of

Bohemia came about largely by accident, or as R. J. W. Evans put it,

> co-existence followed from an uneasy balance of competing forces. Seen in this light, toleration was basically something external: it bespoke a dominance of secular forces and a want – for all the strident importunings from rival clergymen – of deep and divisive piety or commitment.[2]

None the less, the Habsburg rulers of Bohemia and Austria still retained, into the seventeenth century, the notion of the ancient duty to secure a united, Catholic, Holy Roman Empire. As Evans rightly warns, it would be quite wrong for the modern scholar to attempt to make a sharp distinction between religious and political motives in the behaviour of the emperors. They were caught in an intermediate phase between the medieval Empire and what was to become known, from the French Revolution onwards, as the 'Ancien Régime'. In reality, although the Jewish communities in Prague and elsewhere continued to flourish into the seventeenth century, at the same time the Catholic Counter-Reformation was attempting, with strong political backing, to regain ground which had been progressively lost to Protestants, or proto-Protestants, since the fifteenth century. The truth seems to be, however, that the Jews were essentially marginal to this Catholic offensive, though traditional anti-Jewish propaganda continued to be preached with great vigour in Habsburg lands.

The same conclusion may, in general, be drawn from the campaign for the readmission of Jews to England, which reached its height with the Whitehall conference, convened by Cromwell in December 1655. The discussion, by political, religious, and economic leaders, of the possibility of rescinding Edward I's 1290 expulsion order followed a remarkable mission to England by the most prominent leader of the Amsterdam Jewish community, Rabbi Manasseh ben Israel. There had in fact been a few Jews living in the country since at least 1500, most of them refugees from Spain and Portugal, but officially they were Christians. If anything, the flow of such Sephardim had been reduced as a result of the growing attractions of Amsterdam, and those living in England may well have been genuine Christians. Stereotypes of

Jews still, of course, appeared in English literature of the period. Apart from Shylock in Shakespeare's *Merchant of Venice*, there was also Christopher Marlowe's *Jew of Malta*, Barabas, who while representing, like Shylock, the traditional, almost mystical view of the Jew, did also have a few Spanish phrases put into his mouth.[3] David Katz has made meticulous efforts to link Manasseh's mission and the Whitehall conference with the 'philo-Semitic' movements of the first half of the seventeenth-century, such as the quest for a universal language, which many thought to be Hebrew, and eschatalogical ideas associated with the theory that the world would end in 1656. As Abraham Cowley wrote in that year, 'There wants, methinks, but the *Conversion* of . . . the Jews for accomplishing of the kingdom of Christ.'[4] Katz, strangely, omits the long history of such ideas in the Middle Ages, apparently believing them to be a result of the Reformation, but it is none the less undeniable that Manasseh ben Israel was very much influenced in his negotiations by his own messianic ideas, and a belief that England contained Christian sympathizers with his position, when he undertook his mission. However, the paradox of the new, apparently pro-Jewish intellectual currents in England under the Commonwealth and Protectorate has been precisely described by Perry,

> Closer study of the Scriptures by Puritan zealots persuaded many that the Millennium – the return of Christ to earth – would occur only after the conversion of the Jews; Hebrew became the fashionable language to acquire; and for Millenarian theorists Jews ceased to be regarded as bogeymen and came to be seen as strayed but innocent sheep who had to be drawn back into the fold. Some Puritans indeed, seeing themselves as the lost Tribe of Israel, wished to make amends to their brothers the Hebrews for earlier injustice and persecution. Further, the very nonconformity of the Puritans made some of them more tolerant towards Jews, although the tolerance of none extended as far as Papists. There was thus a wave of sympathy, paradoxically called philo-semitism (paradoxically, since it involved the desire to convert the Jews to Christianity and thus put an end to Judaism) although many remained hostile.[5]

Israel has a fairly convincing explanation of the failure of the Whitehall conference, in terms of economic interest. To begin with, he sees Manasseh's mission as 'part of a wider package including the negotiations in Brussels [for the readmission of Jews], and with the dukes of Savoy and Mantua, as well as the schemes for settlement in the Caribbean'.[6] He blames the Dutch rabbi's failure on a combination of entrenched clerical and mercantile interests, which easily overcame the enthusiasm of the Christian 'judaizers'. As Katz himself states, when the moment for decision came, 'Cromwell certainly did not believe that it would be ungodly to readmit the Jews, merely that it was untimely to do so publicly.'[7] However, there were English merchants who wanted to conciliate the Dutch Jews who had so damaged their traffic with the Iberian Peninsula, and Cromwell himself was concerned to expand England's interests in the Caribbean, where Jews based in the Netherlands had such powerful interests. In the event, as Katz states, Jews were indeed allowed to settle in England, but without public approval. The period after the Restoration, however, revealed a conflict between religious and economic considerations, and, in the latter category, a conflict between English merchants and non-mercantile interests. As Josiah Child unkindly commented, 'subtiller the Jews are, and the more trades they pry into while they live here, the more they are like to increase trade, and the more they do that, the better it is for the kingdom in general, though the worse for the English merchant'.[8] In the end, though, the English merchants were forced to accept a certain amount of Jewish competition.

It thus appears that, despite the efforts of some religious people, the Christian edifice had not been breached in such a way as to produce a more positive view of Jews and Judaism among the population at large. The rationalistic intellectual movement which had been begun with Descartes and continued by Spinoza did, eventually, change the attitude of the Gentile majority towards the non-Jewish minority. It is questionable, however, whether the overall result was advantageous to Jews. The clue to what Israel calls 'the new anti-semitism' is already to be found in Spinoza's rejection of the Mosaic Law, including both the Bible itself, and the 'oral Law' or Talmud. Although the Dutch–Jewish philosopher was undoubtedly motivated by disgust at the horrors perpetrated by, and in the name of, religion in his own day, and could hardly have envisaged the attacks on his people which would eventually, three centuries later, be justified to a considerable extent by the ideas of the 'Enlightenment', there is little doubt that he did in reality outline the programme which would be developed, and increasingly followed, in European states after 1700. The problem posed by Spinoza's rejection of ritual and rabbinical Judaism was in due course to be transformed into the late-eighteenth-century demand that Jews should assimilate, if they wished to be freed from the time-honoured burdens and restrictions which were still placed upon them by all early modern states. The situation around the year 1700 was thus delicately balanced. While traditional anti-Judaism, shading into anti-Semitism, was still very much alive, as the Eisenmenger controversy showed, Jews were at the same time beginning to face a new, and in some respects more insidious, threat. Under the new 'Enlightened' dispensation, they were to be offered, for the first time, full citizenship and civil rights, on condition that they gave up all that was unique and distinctive in their religion and culture in the widest sense. The Counter-Reformation, in its slow progress in the remaining Catholic areas, was to carry on medieval anti-Jewish attitudes well into the nineteenth century, but it may be argued that the twentieth century has exposed Enlightenment ideas as the most dangerous threat of all to the survival of Jewry, both socially and as a religion.

The continued co-existence of these two Christian intellectual and practical attitudes to Jews and Judaism into the eighteenth century, reveals the uselessness of attempting to discern a linear or 'progressive' development in relations between Jews and Christians in what had once been 'Catholic' Europe. If there was a kind of 'Golden Age' in seventeenth-century Jewry, as Israel has proposed, it was both temporary and precarious. In some places, it is true, Jews were able to find space in the midst of Gentile confusion to create a more balanced and successful Jewish life, both religious and social, but such developments came about, generally, either as a result of pragmatic decisions or purely by accident. The ability of Gentile Europeans to accept Jews, without particular fear and prejudice, as fellow citizens in the fullest sense, seems to have remained very much at the medieval level. There had always been individuals who, for intellectual or personal reasons, had stepped out of the 'herd', which in this case included people from all social levels, but their influence on overall policy and social attitudes seems to have been scarcely greater in 1700 than it was in 1500. The one major consolation is that, in the midst of fanaticism, cynicism, and violence, so many individuals and even, on occasions, communities, succeeded in leading a full Jewish life in what still generally saw itself as a 'Christian' society.

Notes

1 Jonathan Israel, *European Jewry in the Age of Mercantilism, 1550–1750*, Oxford, Clarendon Press, 1985, p. 175.
2 R. J. W. Evans, *The Making of Habsburg Monarchy 1550–1700*, Oxford, Clarendon Press, 1979, p. 15.
3 Norma Perry, 'Anglo-Jewry, the law, religious conviction, and self-interest (1655–1753)', *Journal of European Studies*, xiv (1984), pp. 1–2, 18.
4 In David Katz, *Philosemitism and the Readmission of the Jews to England, 1603–1655*, Oxford, Clarendon Press, 1982, p. 89.
5 Perry, 'Anglo-Jewry', p. 2.
6 Israel, *European Jewry*, p. 158.
7 Katz, *Philosemitism*, p. 229.
8 Israel, *European Jewry*, p. 160.

Select bibliography

The works mentioned here are intended to provide guidance for the reader to supplement some of the material included in the text. They have not all been specifically cited, and not all works from which material has been directly taken are included. Nearly all the titles are in English.

General

This book owes a very great deal to two works in particular, Salo Wittmayer Baron's massive and magisterial *A Social and Religious History of the Jews*, second, revised edition, New York/Philadelphia, Columbia University Press and Jewish Publication Society of America, 18 volumes to date, 1952–, and Jonathan I. Israel, *European Jewry in the Age of Mercantilism, 1550–1750*, Oxford, Clarendon Press, 1985. Other useful general works are Lionel Kochan, *The Jew and his History*, London, Macmillan, 1977; William Monter, *Ritual, Myth and Magic in Early Modern Europe*, Brighton, Harvester, 1983; Henry Kamen, *The Rise of Toleration*, London, Weidenfeld & Nicolson, 1967; Stephen Sharot, *Judaism. A Sociology*, New York, Holmes & Meier, 1976; *Jewish Thought in the Sixteenth Century*, ed Bernard Dov Cooperman, Cambridge, Mass., Harvard University Press, 1983.

   As well as the above, the following works relate to the individual chapters.

Introduction

William A. Christian, Jr, *Local Religion in Sixteenth-Century Spain*, Princeton University Press, 1981; J. H. Edwards, 'The *conversos*: a theological approach', *Bulletin of Hispanic Studies*, lxii (1985), 39–49; both works discuss the theoretical and practical implications of the Spanish evidence.

Chapter 1

For the medieval background:
John Gager, *The Origins of Anti-Semitism*, New York, Oxford University Press, 1983; Solomon Grayzel, *The Church and the Jews in the Thirteenth Century*, Philadelphia, Jewish Publication Society of America, 1933; Jeremy Cohen, *The Friars and the Jews: the Evolution of Medieval Anti-Judaism*, Ithaca and London, Cornell University Press, 1982; Joshua Trachtenberg, *The Devil and the Jews*, New Haven, Yale University Press, 1943; on millenarianism and apocalyptic, Norman Cohn, *The Pursuit of the Millennium: Revolutionary Millenarians and Mystical Anarchists of the Middle Ages*, London, Secker & Warburg, 1957; for pictorial evidence, Thérèse and Mendel Metzger, *Jewish Life in the Middle Ages. Illuminated Hebrew Manuscripts of the Thirteenth to the Sixteenth centuries*, New York, Alpine Fine Arts Collection, 1982.
On Spain:
Philippe Wolff, 'The 1391 pogrom in Spain. Social crisis or not?', *Past and Present*, 50 (1971), pp. 4–18; Angus MacKay, 'Popular movements and pogroms in fifteenth-century Castile', *Past and Present*, 55 (1972), pp. 33–67; Roger Highfield, 'Christians, Jews and Muslims in the same society: the fall of *convivencia* in medieval Spain', *Studies in Church History*, xv, ed D. Baker, Oxford, Blackwell, 1977, pp. 125–37; J. H. Edwards, 'Religious belief and social conformity: the *converso* problem in late-medieval Córdoba', *Transactions of the Royal Historical Society*, 5th series, xxxi (1981), pp. 115–28; the best short account of the expulsion is Maurice Kriegel, 'La prise d'une décision: l'expulsion des Juifs d'Espagne en 1492', *Revue Historique*, cclx (1968), pp. 49–90. For a good general survey of late medieval communities around the Mediterranean, see Kriegel's, *Les Juifs à la fin du Moyen Age dans l'Europe méditerranéenne*, Paris, Hachette, 1979.

Chapter 2

For Kabbalah, Cabbala and other Renaissance religion and magic: Frances Yates, *Giordano Bruno and the Hermetic Tradition*, London, Routledge & Kegan Paul, 1964: D. P. Walker, *Spiritual and Demonic Magic from Ficino to Campanella*, London, Warburg Institute 1958, repr. Neudeln/Liechtenstein, Kraus, 1969; on Jewish mysticism, Gershom Scholem, *Major Trends in Jewish Mysticism*, New York and Jerusalem, various editions, 1941– ; Kabbalistic texts from Safed in English translation in *Safed Spirituality*, ed Lawrence Fine, New York, Paulist Press, London, SPCK, 1984; on the Reformers' attitudes to Jews, see the important essay by Heiko A. Oberman in *Jewish Thought in the Sixteenth Century*.

Chapter 3

The main work on Papal Jewish policy is Kenneth R. Stow, *Catholic Thought and Papal Jewish Policy, 1555–1593*, New York, Jewish Theological Seminary of America, 1977. The best modern studies of Italian Jewish communities are, Ariel Toaff, *The Jews in Medieval Assisi, 1305–1487. A Social and Economic History of a Small Jewish Community in Italy*, Florence, Olschki, 1979; Shlomo Simonsohn, *History of the Jews in the Duchy of Mantua*, Jerusalem, Ktav, 1977, and, as editor, *The Jews in the Duchy of Milan*, 2 vols, Jerusalem, Israel Academy of Sciences and Humanities, 1982; M. A. Shulvass, *The Jews in the World of the Renaissance*, Leiden, Brill, 1973; Michele Luzzati, *La Casa dell'Ebreo. Saggi sugli Ebrei a Pisa e in Toscana nel Medioevo e nel Rinascimento*, Pisa, Nistri-Lischi, 1985. On Venice, there are many articles by Brian Pullan, his major full-length works being, *Rich and Poor in Renaissance Venice. The Social Institutions of a Catholic State to 1620*, Oxford, Blackwell, 1971, and *The Jews of Europe and the Inquisition of Venice, 1550–1670*, Oxford, Blackwell, 1983.

On Rome, see Léon Poliakov, *Jewish Bankers and the Holy See, from the Thirteenth to the Seventeenth Centuries*, London, Routledge, 1967.

Chapter 4

The best general account of the Dutch revolt is now the revised edition of Geoffrey Parker, *The Dutch Revolt*, rev. edn, Harmondsworth, Penguin, 1985. In addition, Phyllis Mack Crew, *Calvinist Preaching and Iconoclasm in the Netherlands, 1544–1569*, Cambridge, Cambridge University Press, 1978 is a useful study of the religious context, while Israel is the master of the economic activity of Dutch Jewry. See, in particular, 'The economic contribution of Dutch Sephardi Jewry to Holland's golden age, 1598–1713', in *Tijdschrift voor Geschiedenis*, xcvi (1983), and his essay, 'The changing role of the Dutch Sephardim in international trade, 1595–1715', in *Dutch Jewish History*, a collection of papers from an Israeli seminar, edited by Jozeph Mishman and Tirtsah Levie (Leiden, Brill, 1984). The sources on the Amsterdam community are being edited in extract and calendar form by the Amsterdam municipal archivists, and published in sections in *Studia Rosenthaliana*, from vol. i (1967–).

On Jews under Habsburg rule, the important specific works are by R. J. W. Evans, *The Making of the Habsburg Monarchy, 1550–1700*, Oxford, Clarendon Press, 1979 and, on cultural history, *Rudolph II and his World*, Oxford, Clarendon Press, 1973. A study of a leading figure of Prague Jewry is Byron L. Sherwin, *Mystical Theology and Social Dissent: the Life and Works of Judah Loew of Prague*, London, Associated University Presses, 1982.

On Poland, there is a collection of general early modern papers, *A Republic of Nobles. Studies in Polish History to 1864*, edited by J. K. Federowicz, Maria Bogucka, and Henryk Samsonowicz, Cambridge, Cambridge University Press, 1982, containing useful essays by Maczak, Geremek, Zientara, Wyczanski and Tazbir. See also the last's *A State without Stakes. Polish Religious Toleration in the Sixteenth and Seventeenth Centuries*, New York, Twayne, 1973. Norman Davies's *God's Playground. A History of Poland in Two Volumes*, vol. i, *The Origins to 1795*, Oxford, Clarendon Press, 1973, should be consulted.

However, the most useful recent material on Jewish history is the collection of papers from a 1984 Oxford conference, edited by Chimen Abramsky, Maciej Jachimczyk and Antony Polonsky, under the title *The Jews in Poland*, Oxford, Blackwell, 1986. Particularly useful are the contributions by Gieysztor, Tollet, Goldberg and Hundert.

Chapter 5

Works of a general kind, and those on Italy, the Netherlands and Poland, have already been referred to in previous sections. However, there should be special reference, while the translation from the Hebrew of his study of Isaac Orobio de Castro is still awaited, to Yosef Kaplan's studies, 'The social functions of the *herem* in the Portuguese Jewish community of Amsterdam in the seventeenth century', in *Dutch Jewish History* (see section on chapter 4 above), and 'The travels of Portuguese Jews from Amsterdam to the "Lands of Idolatry" (1644–1724)', in *Jews and Conversos. Studies in Society and the Inquisition*, ed. Kaplan, Jerusalem, Magnes Press, 1984. For a study of the long-term history of a small Jewish community in French papal territory, see Marianne Calmann, *The Carrière of Carpentras*, Oxford University Press, 1984.

Chapter 6

On the medieval background, R. I. Moore, *The Origins of European Dissent*, revised edition, Oxford, Blackwell, 1985. For the sixteenth century, Lucien Febvre, *The Problem of Unbelief in the Sixteenth Century. The Religion of Rabelais*, Cambridge, Mass., Harvard University Press, 1982, is the seminal work. For an inspiring modern study, see Carlo Ginzburg, *The Cheese and the Worms. The Cosmos of a Sixteenth-century Miller*, London, Routledge & Kegan Paul, 1980. On Bodin, see Paul Lawrence Rose, *Bodin and the Great God of Nature*, Geneva, Droz, 1980. For developments in Judaism, see the work of the sociologist Stephen Sharot, 'Jewish millenarianism: a comparison of medieval communities', *Comparative Studies in Society and History*, xxii (1980), pp. 394–415. The magisterial study of Sabbatai Sevi and his movement is Gershom Scholem, *Sabbatai Sevi, the Mystical Messiah (1626–1676)*, Princeton, Princeton University Press, 1973. *The Hope of Israel*, an important text by the Dutch Jewish leader Menasseh ben Israel, has been edited with a full introduction by Henry Méchoulan and Gérard Nahon (Oxford, Oxford University Press, 1987).

Chapter 7

Apart from those already referred to in earlier sections, there are two useful works on the readmission of Jews to England: David Katz, *Philosemitism and the Readmission of the Jews to England, 1603–1655*, Oxford, Clarendon Press, 1982, and Norma Perry, 'Anglo-Jewry, the law, religious conviction, and self-interest (1655–1753)', *Journal of European Studies*, xiv (1984), pp. 1–23.

Index